MW01042232

The Public Relations Writing Exercise Book

Bob J. Carrell
University of Oklahoma

Doug A. Newsom
Texas Christian University

Wadsworth Publishing Company
Belmont, California

A Division of Wadsworth, Inc.

Production Notes

This book was written, composed and designed by Bob J. Carrell and Doug A. Newsom on an Apple© Macintosh™ Classic, using Microsoft© Word™ (Version 4.0) and Excel™ (Version 2.2), Aldus© PageMaker™ (Version 4.01) and Sensible Grammar™. Camera-ready pages were produced on a NewGen© TurboPS/400p™ laser printer.

1 2 3 4 5 6 7 8 9 10 — 96 95 94 93 92

Contents

List of Tables

List of Examples

Preface

Epictetus, a Stoic philosopher in the golden age of Greece, once said if you want to be a writer, write. That advice is still valuable. You can learn about good writing by reading the works of good writers. And you can learn a lot from professors and from textbooks. But nothing substitutes for the actual practice of writing. Practice may not make you a perfect writer, but it can make you a better writer.

We chose to call this book *The Public Relations Writing Exercise Book* for two reasons. First, we wanted the title to be fully descriptive of the book's content and purpose. Second, we wanted the term *exercise* in the title to highlight the concept of writing practice. Like superb athletes, gifted writers practice, practice, practice.

The Public Relations Writing Exercise Book helps you work independently on your writing or in concert with the ideas and skills to which you are introduced in a formal course. If you are presently enrolled in a public relations writing class, you may be using our third edition of *Public Relations Writing: Form & Style.* This book is coordinated with that text. We hope you find they go well together. You'll find references in this book to that text. For example, instructions in an assignment might begin with "Refer to *PRW3e*, p. 321f, for some background on how to do this assignment." That is a suggestion to turn to page 321 and read it and the following pages for help before you tackle the assignment.

Writing with Purpose

Learning to be a good public relations writer is learning to write with purpose. It isn't enough simply to master the mechanics of grammar, spelling and punctuation. They rank with learning to touch-type so you can produce prose on a typewriter or a word processor. Although these skills are important, they're technical skills. They only deal with the form of your writing, not its substance.

A Goal and Six Rules

The goal of every piece of public relations writing is to get others to think or do something you want them to think or do. Such a task calls for high levels of preparation and strategic and creative thinking before you ever write a line. You must concentrate on six simple rules:

1. Understand your audience thoroughly.

2. Identify what is relevant to your audience, and why.

3. Match the message you want to send to the needs of your audience as your audience sees them, not as you perceive them.

4. Write a message acceptable to your audience.

5. Send your message through media to which your audience pays attention.

6. Deliver the message at the right time and as often as necessary to get it across.

If you always observe these six rules, your chances of becoming an effective public relations writer will improve eventually. We add that qualifier because we don't know how serious you really are about think-time.

Think-Time

Think-time is the time you spend digging for information, analyzing and conceptualizing it and asking all sorts of "What if?" questions. It also includes the time you spend in rewriting a message until you write it right. Good writers spend most writing time as think-time.

Effective think-time requires self-discipline. Look at those six rules again. Only number four deals with the act of writing. The rest are concerned with thinking, analyzing, preparing to write and making decisions about to whom, when, how and how often messages will be delivered. Many beginning public relations writers ignore or forget those other five rules. They simply want to get on with the writing task. "I'm getting paid to write, not to be a researcher, planner or thinker. I just want to write."

We applaud the compulsion to fill blank pages. But we must ask, with what? Effective public relations writers deal with substance first and form second. It is simply an issue of priorities. Only when you are willing to prepare for writing will your wordsmithing skills pay off. The preparation we're talking about is going to be boring sometimes. But think-time can produce exciting results if you use it well. These ideas have led us to organize and structure this exercise book as we have.

Organization and Structure

All exercises and situations in this book happen in Serene, a fictional community in Serendipity County, USA. Read and study the information about Serene. Refer to it as often as necessary when you work with the exercises. If you wish, substitute your community for Serene, but please keep the organizations, issues, problems and situations in the exercises intact—as though they are happening in your community.

The Quick-Study page that precedes each new set of exercises is a digest of information you should review thoroughly before trying the exercises. These digests summarize principles, points and issues drawn from chapters in the third edition of *Public Relations Writing: Form & Style*. Refer to that book for more detailed information.

Four scenarios are described before you get into the first set of exercises. Each scenario presents basic information you must refer to regularly, depending on which exercises you choose or which ones are assigned. Later exercises present new information and situations you must integrate into the context of the ongoing scenario.

The primary data in the first scenario are accurate, plausible. However, the bank, market and situation are fictional. The other scenarios also are fictional, but they are no less real in the sense that they are built around existing sources and similar situations. They represent an amalgamation of information and issues that we hope you find challenging and fun.

We urge you to work through the exercises related to one scenario. A scenario leads you through a broad range of writing tasks. And when you finish, you'll have a well-coordinated package of written materials that clearly shows how you can adapt your writing skills from one situation to another. You'll have a portfolio, "clips" if you will, that will make a good impression on potential employers.

If you prefer to work with independent assignments, you'll find them in each section. These exercises are effective when you're trying to learn the art of writing itself. But we're convinced you'll learn more about the central role good writing plays in public relations if you do the exercises related to a particular scenario.

You'll also find that think-time governs most of your success as a writer. Use your think-time wisely and you'll write with confidence and skill. Occasionally, you'll have to go to the library or consult other resources to get the information you need to handle some assignments with finesse.

In summary, then:

1. Research your subject and your audience.

2. Keep your audience and the medium in mind as you write.

3. Rewrite and polish.

4. Keep your language tools well honed.

5. And as Epictetus would no doubt have it: Write every day.

Special Thanks

Books are rarely the works only of the people named on title pages. That is certainly true of this book. We owe debts of thanks to many people for their help and inspiration. Among them are Kris Clerkin, editor, and Gerald Holloway, production services manager, both at Wadsworth Publishing Company, Belmont, California; Phyllis Miller, University of Arkansas, Fayetteville, Arkansas and Shirley Ramsey, University of Oklahoma, Norman, Oklahoma.

We especially salute David L. Sturges of the University of Texas-Pan American, Edinburg, Texas for his many ideas related to the scenarios. We also thank all the students who served as willing "guinea pigs" as we tested some of the assignments. Their insights and comments were invaluable.

Bob Carrell and Doug Newsom

Getting Started

Preparing to write is the critical first step in learning how to write well. Writing well in public relations is learning to write with careful attention given to a piece of writing's purpose and context. Context is what this section on getting started is about. Study the material below. It introduces you to fictional organizations, situations and people who interact to form a fictional community. As you study them, try to picture them clearly. Some are admirable. Others aren't. But many play major or minor roles in some exercises you will do.

Serene, Serendipity County, U.S.A.

The 1990 census counted Serene's population at 150,012, but Serendipity County has a population of 202,112. Serene is also the county seat. Serene provides goods and services for three counties with a combined population of 295,435. Because the main campus of State University also is located here, Serene is the commercial and educational hub of the southcentral part of the state. Although Serene has some light industrial manufacturers, its recent growth has been spurred mostly by high-tech research and development firms and manufacturers attracted to an abundance of electronic and business expertise available at the university.

Serene is connected to several metropolitan areas by north-south and east-west interstate highways, although the nearest major market is 106 miles away. The city is surrounded by rich agricultural land. Some mining goes on, but it has declined sharply over the last 20 years. In 1960, 31 percent of all jobs in the Serene area were related to mining; now that figure is only two percent. Amtrak provides regular rail service and Peaceful Airport, 12 minutes north by car from downtown, provides nine round-trip flights daily to two hub airports. Community leaders have had a difficult time, especially in the last 10 years, providing city services because Serenites have sometimes balked at appropriating new taxes and approving municipal bonds.

Mass Media and Agencies

Serene has a good selection of media for a market its size. The *Clarion* is an evening daily newspaper with Saturday morning and Sunday editions. Its format is full-size standard advertising unit (SAU). See the Appendix for an explanation of SAU. The *Clarion's* Sunday circulation averaged 89,323 in 1991 but the Monday to Saturday issues averaged 81,011. About 77 percent of the *Clarion's* circulation is within Serene city limits. It also offers a total market coverage (TMC) package. The living and food sections are wrapped in a four-page news section and mailed to every non-subscriber household in the three-county trade territory for Thursday delivery.

The *Free Press* is a weekly newspaper with an average circulation of 8,689 in 1990. About 70 percent of its circulation is outside Serene city limits. Its strengths are its reports from rural correspondents, areawide school news and sports and coverage of the activities of county governments, especially road commissioners.

Radio Stations

Four radio stations originate signals in Serene. KICU-AM-FM is the state university station affiliated with National Public Radio (NPR). It takes most NPR feeds and originates some jazz and classical music programs. It also airs a one-hour rock music program daily at 10 P.M. that focuses on new artists, styles and albums. KICU news has won several reporting awards for aggressive pursuit of stories by student trainees.

KARY-AM is a dawn-to-dusk operation that programs country-western music, but its news and sports are mostly rip-and-read. It does a superb job of reporting agricultural news, including markets and weather forecasts.

KSKY-AM-FM is a 24-hour station that has a blend of light and easy listening music, interspersed with five-minute news segments, weather and sports on the hour. Its daily (no Sunday) 7 A.M. hour-long newscast is a wrap-up of overnight news locally and global news. Its daily (no Sunday) 30-minute noon newscast focuses on news from Washington, D.C., the state capital and Wall Street, including some brief market summaries. Its 6 P.M. hour-long newscast covers local, state, national and international news. As appropriate to the season, KSKY carries live intercollegiate sporting events in which State University teams compete. It is the most listened-to station by people 35 years or older.

KISS-FM operates from 6 A.M. to midnight. Its programming is mostly rock, with some heavy metal thrown in. It does three rip-and-read, 15-minute newscasts daily, at 6 A.M., 11:45 A.M. and 6:45 P.M. It carries some talk shows that focus on music, musicians and other social icons.

Television Stations

Two television stations serve the area. One is the university-owned KICU-TV, Channel 13 (VHF), affiliated with the Public Broadcasting System (PBS). It does Monday to Friday, 30-minute magazine format newscasts that focus on university and Serene events.

The other television station is an independent, KWIK-TV, which broadcasts on Channel 25 (UHF). It does a 30-minute newscast at 7 A.M., noon, 6 P.M. and 10 P.M. Each consists of about 13 minutes of news and features, 5 minutes of weather and 7 minutes of sports. Three 30-minute talk shows on Sunday depend on callers to question guests. One show focuses on city government and schools, another on economics and politics and the third on social services and issues.

A subsidiary of the Serene Telephone Company is the local cable outlet, Serene Cable Company (SCC), which imports and redistributes signals from 18 other sources, including ABC, CBS, NBC, ESPN, TNT, Fox, Showtime (SHOW), Cinemax (MAX) and Arts and Entertainment (A&E). Additionally, SCC provides a public access channel (Channel 34, UHF) on which city council and school board meetings and the like are aired regularly. Serene's two public high schools also are hooked into the cable company. The schools provide some programs (most are taped) created with equipment supplied by SCC.

Public Relations and Advertising Agencies

Three agencies are located in Serene. One is Ideas, Inc., started four years ago by B. G. Deas. Ideas, Inc. employs a combination writer-designer and a secretary. It has made unsuccessful pitches to some regional advertising and public relations accounts, but the agency seems to survive, but barely, on local advertising accounts and an occasional public relations job.

Clever Words, Inc., is another agency that seems to focus on accounts that need publicity and on special events. Cleve R. Word edited the local weekly for 10 years before he founded the agency in 1968. Most of Word's accounts are local, but the agency has done some regional promotions and special events over the last five years. The agency has six employees. Word is the president. Clever Words has two account executives, one an excellent writer, the other a talented designer and a production artist. There are two junior writers, neither of whom seems to be inspired, and a secretary.

Professional Communication Consultants, Inc. (ProCom)

Professional Communication Consultants, Inc. (ProCom) has operated in Serene the last nine years. It is owned and headed by I. M. Professor. She or he is your professor, who may prefer to be called by her or his proper name. She or he is dedicated to providing ProCom clients with the best service possible.

Although ProCom has just 20 employees, including Professor as president, the agency has a successful track record. It not only serves the Serene business community, but it also has several regional accounts and four national accounts. It is affiliated with a network of agencies in some major markets around the country. A client could hardly want a service that ProCom can't provide in-house or with the support of an affiliate.

Professor is good at developing new accounts, especially with the support of Kari M. Backe who serves as executive vice president and account services supervisor. She has 20 years of account service work to her credit, having worked for major agencies in Los Angeles, Seattle, Chicago, Kansas City and New York City before joining ProCom eight years ago. Benjamin A. Counter has been vice president of finance and operations for two years. Professor hired him two years ago. Counter ran a plumbing supply house for six years before joining ProCom.

ProCom's Writers

ProCom also employs five account executives, four writers (three of whom are junior writers—*you are one of them*), two designers, a production artist, a broadcast and audiovisual specialist and four secretaries. Professor says ProCom soon will add two positions, director of research and senior writer.

Professor is regarded highly in many large-market agencies, and they steal away some of their best creative talent from ProCom. Professor often complains ProCom is a training ground for the success of others, but Professor has such a commitment to helping young people start careers that these complaints are really expressions of pride.

Serene Chamber of Commerce

The Serene Chamber of Commerce has won several state and some national awards because of a very active membership. Although he is a long-time member of the Chamber, Richard R. Wilde, vice president for operations at Tentative Electronics, Inc., has been Chamber president just two months.

The first vice president is Glennis A. Klose. She is chief legal counsel at State University. Second vice president is Harry H. Usury, president of First American Bank. The Chamber's treasurer is Hiram M. Walker, owner and operator of The Serene Palace, a local nightspot that draws its customers mostly from the State University campus. The Chamber executive secretary is Ima H. Worker. She's held this spot 13 years.

The chairs of three major committees are Heddon T. Clouds, Economic Development Committee, A. W. Happy, Special Events Committee and Justin J. Joiner, Membership Committee.

Serene City Council

The City Council has six ward seats from which the mayor is elected by council members present and voting. The mayoral term is two years. Ward terms are for three years, and are staggered so two incumbents face reelection every year. Chairing the council for his third consecutive term is Darien W. Dorsey, who's in the first year of his fourth term representing Ward 6. Dorsey owns and operates the Serene Lincoln, Mercury and Ford dealership, a family business he inherited 15 years ago. Before that he served six years as sales director for a clothing manufacturer on the East Coast.

Purl E. Maye, who represents Ward 1, is a homemaker. She's devoted much of her time to volunteer service at the Serene Regional Hospital and to United Way. She headed the UW drive last year and exceeded its goal by 11 percent. She also sits on the Board of Directors of a major diversified energy company, Envire, Inc., whose subsidiaries include oil and gas exploration, pipeline operations, a state utility and processing and distribution divisions. She's fond of saying that she was invited onto the board "as a token because I'm black, but not beautiful. I was quick to say yes, baby, because somebody's got to keep those honkies honest. It might as well be me." She gets things done. Perhaps that's why she's in her fourth term on the council.

Kary M. Backus represents Ward 2 and is in his first term. He owns and operates KARY-AM radio. He came to Serene eight years ago from the West Coast, where he was sales manager for a major line of heating and air-conditioning duct materials and supplies.

William (Bill) Belcher is in his second term from Ward 3. Belcher is Serene's leading restaurateur. He operates Strawberry Lake, noted for its nouvelle cuisine, and he has managers to run Pig Out, famous for its babyback ribs, and Abbaraccio (meaning "to embrace"), known for its northern Italian dishes. Belcher also owns 49 percent of three McDonald's franchises in Serene.

Tulley Howard Ho (his close friends call him Tally Ho) is a first-generation Vietnamese-American whose passion is agriculture and horses. He has accumulated several hundred acres around Serene where he has farming and horse operations (mostly thoroughbreds, but some quarter horses). He represents Ward 4. Because of the bloodlines, Ho's horse auctions draw major breeders and buyers from across the nation. He is in his second term on the council.

Robert N. Robbins, Ward 5, spends his full time managing his diversified investments portfolio, although he does consent to some financial consulting now and then. He inherited much of his holdings from his grandfather, who owned the Serene First Federal Savings and Loan for 42 years. The grandfather committed suicide when SFFS&L became insolvent four years ago. Robbins is in his first term on the council. As he's only 29, some council members disregard his opinions.

Serene School Board

The Serene School Board has six members. They serve three-year staggered terms. The president is elected for a one-year term by board members present and voting. The board supervises 2 public high schools (grades 11 and 12), 4 junior high schools (grades 9 and 10), 8 middle schools (grades 7 and 8) and 20 elementary schools (kindergarten through grade 6). The board in recent years has been sharply divided on issues of school size, financing and operating policies. However, these conflicts are smoothed over so the board seems harmonious to the public.

Oscar T. House is in his third term on the board, but it is his second as president. He is president of Tentative Electronics, Inc. (TEI), a small but growing manufacturer of electronics equipment and supplies used in the financial community nationwide. Its over-the-counter stock uses the NASDAQ symbol TEI and closed yesterday at $2 per share. Ector S. Million is in his fourth term as a school board member. He is vice president of operations at the Serene National Bank.

Pauline B. Pundus is in the second year of her first term. She is currently president of the local chapter of Daughters of the American Revolution (DAR). Ms. Pundus's family settled in the Serene area more than 150 years ago. She earned her doctorate in American Studies at the University of Minnesota, but her other degrees in humanities are from the State University in Serene. Her fiancé was killed in an automobile accident 28 years ago, 48 hours before their wedding day, and she has never married. At 52, she lives alone on the family estate with her dog, Blossom, a frisky Boston Terrier. Pundus Avenue is one of Serene's main downtown streets and Pundus Park, southwest of central Serene, is named for her father.

Esther Little-Deere is an attorney married to Marcus F. Deere, also an attorney. She runs the staff of the public defender's office. She's in her first term on the board. Unsubstantiated rumors claim she wants to be district attorney, so she can use that job as a stepping stone to a statewide post.

Robert N. Jester owns and operates the Serene Comedy Club and Bar. He is not taken seriously by other board members, even though he's in his third term. Alan A. Sellers is the advertising director of KWIK-TV. He's in the first year of his first term on the board. He's generally regarded as a "young man to watch" because of his brains, drive and persistence.

Serene Politicians

U.S. Senator Herchel H. Hanzout lives in Serene. Although some say he's not well liked by his constituents, he has beaten all challengers and has been in Washington 14 years. He now chairs the powerful Ways and Means Committee. The family has been in politics for decades, although Herchel is the first Hanzout to serve in Washington. His father served two terms as governor and his grandfather was speaker of the State House of Representatives for 22 years. Hanzout earned his baccalaureate degree (BA) in political science from Princeton and has a Master of Business Administration degree (MBA) from Harvard.

He was a third-year law student when he quit to run his first Senate race. Hanzout's wife, Paula, is a sister to Pauline Pundus. Mrs. Hanzout was educated at Vassar and studied art for three years at the Sorbonne. They have three children, two of whom are married and live out of state. The youngest attends State University. She is a fifth-year senior with a double major in public relations and classics and minors in computer science and statistics.

State Representative P. N. Barrell also lives in Serene and is in his sixth term. He represents Serendipity County and a small section of an adjoining county. He serves on several important committees, but, according to him, he's declined chairing any of them because he prefers to work "behind the scenes." He has cosponsored several controversial bills, some of which became law, but he's never authored a bill himself.

He worked his way through college and law school. He has made a name for himself as a tough defense attorney, who has successfully defended people in several celebrated criminal cases. Although he's only 48, he's amassed in the last 15 years an estate estimated to be worth over $20,000,000. He dresses flamboyantly and has married and divorced three times. His marriages have produced no offspring, but he's rumored to be the father of two, a boy 11 and a girl 6, each with a different mother.

Personal Notes about Serene -

Scenario 1—
First National Bank

First National Bank (FNB) is one of the old-line banks in Serene. It was one of three banks located in midtown for several decades. Serene's other two banks are Second National Bank (SNB) and First State Bank (FSB). Market growth prompted two new competitors to enter the market in 1974, First American Bank (FAB), operating with a state charter, and Exchange National Bank (ENB). Further growth saw Commerce State Bank (CSB) chartered in 1985. The newest competitor is Republic Federal Bank (RFB), set to begin operations with a national charter next July.

Because branch banking is now permissible, FNB opened a branch on the town's northwest side in 1986. The area is rapidly developing with middle-class, single-family housing, and the branch is readily accessible to residents in more affluent Serene neighborhoods. Both SNB and FSB opened branches, too, but SNB's branch is opposite FNB at the same intersection. The FSB branch is on the east side of town. All banks now have 24-hour electronic teller services.

Dramatic Changes

Changes in state banking laws resulting from deregulation in the 1980s have altered the market dramatically. Not only do new banks represent more direct competition to FNB, but so do savings and loans and credit unions, which can now offer many services traditionally available only at banks.

FNB management is painfully aware that the Serene market has become troubled in the last few years, especially with the spillover effects from so many bank failures nationally, including three locally, and the savings and loan debacle. FNB has had a marketing department for many years, but its primary functions were to place advertising in local media and to conduct occasional special promotions to lure new accounts. Because of the perceived lack of expertise on the bank's staff, FNB has hired your firm, Professional Communication Consultants (ProCom), to do a communications audit of current policies and practices and to recommend a communication plan the bank can follow into the next century.

ProCom's Secondary Research

ProCom's research efforts have already produced data for your use in the audit. The latest bank calls (statements of financial conditions that must be published in the local newspaper at the close of each operating quarter) may give you a sense of what is going on in Serene-area banking right now. For example, Table S1-1 shows total deposits for all banks. Note that FNB held a 32 percent market share in 1970, but only 19 percent share at the end of 1991.

This drop can be rationalized easily by looking at FNB's time deposits, which have grown by 2,999 percent in the same 22-year period. But a check of the last column shows that time deposits in all banks increased by 4,034 percent. Increased competition could account for the share loss; however, SNB shows only a 3 percent drop in market share over the same period. This may only mean that SNB was doing a more aggressive job of promoting itself than was FNB.

Demand and Time Deposits

Demand deposits (those that can be withdrawn at any time without penalty), shown in Table S1-2, reveal much the same thing. FNB had lost 8 percent of its market share by 1991, but FSB had gained a percentage point. Apparently FNB felt the effect of increased competition more than the other banks. The bank with the most success in gaining market share of total demand deposits was FAB which grew from 13 percent to 21 percent.

When time and demand deposits are combined (Table S1-3), they profile total deposits in all Serene banks. FNB lost 10 percent of its market share during the period, although that's somewhat better than SNB's loss of 15 percent. FSB kept its loss to only 7 percent of market share. FAB now has 18 percent, ENB 6 percent and CSB 9 percent.

When FAB and ENB entered the market in 1975, their combined efforts quickly accounted for 22.7 percent of bank assets (Table S1-4), some of which came from FNB. But the most aggressive of all the banks has been CSB, which in six years claimed 8.6 percent of the total assets. FSB seems to have protected itself better than FNB and SNB, losing only 4.7 percent in asset share.

ProCom's data were used to create indexes for each bank, shown in Table S1-5. These indexes may help you to see some relationships among banks' performances. Because CSB didn't enter the market until 1986 the ProCom researchers used 1989 as the base year. That choice is more recent than is desirable but ProCom can't rewrite history. FNB's index suggests it is on a positive course compared to SNB, FSB and FAB. The index for ENB is impressive, but closer examination of other tables shows ENB has been languishing for years. Since CSB has been a competitor for such a short time, its index is best ignored because short-term growth, when compared to long-term growth on the same base, is magnified in an index.

Loan Share

FNB has a clearly conservative philosophy regarding loans. Of course, one way banks make money is to lend money and charge interest on it. Profitability is related to the difference between interest rates at which money is loaned and paid on deposits. If loans are not sound and can't be collected or collected for only cents on the dollar, then banks lose money. Hence, if enough bad loans are made, not only are a bank's profits endangered but also the safety of depositors' money is threatened. Table S1-6 compares FNB with the competition.

FNB and SNB were tied with 30 percent of market share in 1970. FSB was 10 points ahead. Because of economic changes in the 1970s and 1980s, FNB became more conservative in loan practices than it had been in the previous years. Its loan market share had fallen to 10 per cent by 1988. But the bank closed 1991 at a 14 percent share. SNB seems to have followed a similar pattern. However, FSB continued to loan at high levels, closing 1991 just three points below its historic high of 40 percent. The other banks seem not to have been affected much during this time period.

Loan practices alone do not provide a complete picture of a bank's activity. A bank's capital position must also be analyzed to get an indication of its strength and how easily it can absorb bad loans. Table S1-7 shows that FNB has increased its capital over the last few years so it now controls 24 percent of the total market, a larger share than all other banks except FSB, which has a relative capital loss of 9 percent. This suggests that FNB is relatively strong as a banking institution, but how strong?

Strength

One way to answer that question is to look at the capital-to-loan (debt-to-equity) ratios. These ratios are shown in Table S1-8.

Banks generally should maintain a ratio of one dollar for each six to eight dollars lent. This guideline is suggested to accomplish two essential purposes:

1. A bank that exercises ordinary prudence in evaluating loan applications can make loans at this ratio without endangering the safety of depositors' money.

2. Loans made within this range generally allow sufficient economic safety without cutting off local sources of capital to finance community growth and development. At the same time, this guideline is used to warn banks that if they chronically lend at ratios of less than 1:6, they are unlikely to make enough money to pay savers competitive interest rates. Hence deposits may decline; therefore, less money is available for loans.

Table S1-8 shows that FNB has the best record of complying with the guideline. Because of a rash of bad loans, SNB, FSB, ENB and CSB are operating outside the recommended ratios. FAB was also for a time in non-compliance, but has brought its ratio almost back to the upper limits of the acceptable range.

ProCom's researchers constructed a final table (Table S1-9) that summarizes all pertinent information for 1991. This table includes some information previously discussed, but it also includes additional financial ratios such as capital-to-deposits, equity-to-assets and loans-to-deposits. In general, FNB has better ratios than the other banks.

Objective

After reviewing this information, what conclusions can you draw about the operations of FNB? Its philosophy? Its mission?

Close examination of FNB accounts shows that approximately 80 percent of profits come from 20 percent of its customers. Many of these accounts are held by retailers, manufacturers, service organizations and professional people (doctors, dentists, CPAs, engineers and the like). Only about 20 percent of the bank's profits come from the remaining 80 percent of depositors. The cost-effectiveness of this last group of accounts is marginal. In fact, some accounts are so small that service fees charged sometimes don't cover the costs of handling them. Hence, FNB management has already set one marketing objective: to attract more accounts in the cost-effective category.

FNB management is also deeply troubled by the wave of bank and savings and loan insolvencies plaguing the country. Locally, the effect of an uninsured savings and loan's bankruptcy four years ago has led to ongoing litigation extensively reported in the media, all of which perpetuates fears and misunderstanding about current conditions in banking in the Serene area. In addition, four banks (SNB, FSB, FAB and ENB) in Serene have been acquired over the last five years by major bank-holding companies, although insolvency was not the catalyst in one (FAB) such acquisition.

ProCom's Primary Research

After ProCom's team consulted extensively with FNB management, ProCom researchers conducted a survey of current attitudes about banks in general and banks in Serene in particular. ProCom researchers followed these steps:

1. They reviewed the data from the bank call analysis to confirm or modify evidence about the financial condition of Serene banks.

2. They talked to employees and managers in most of the banks in Serene as well as a few people at three other banks in the trade territory.

3. They spent time in the library reading everything they could about banking in the U.S., state and Serene banking. They focused especially on how best to promote banks, trends in bank failures and on public perceptions of banks.

Following this search of secondary sources, ProCom researchers concluded that some primary research must be done to measure attitudes and opinions of local residents. This step seemed especially important because of the public's perceptions that the banking and savings and loan industries were in turmoil. ProCom got authorization from FNB's management to spend the money for this research—but it wasn't easy because primary research doesn't come cheap!

Telephone Survey

The ProCom team decided a telephone questionnaire would generate the needed information and would be the most cost-effective method. A questionnaire was designed with a target of 10 minutes as the maximum time to complete a phone interview. It took three meetings to reach consensus with FNB management on what should be included in the questionnaire and how the questions would be asked.

A pretest of the questionnaire discovered that some questions were too difficult to understand, especially among people whose language of choice was not English. A few questions were modified to make them clearer for use on the telephone. A set number of completed interviews was agreed upon to ensure the sample was representative of the Serene population as a whole. Three hundred ninety-eight interviews were completed with respondents in households selected at random between 4:40 P.M. and 8:30 P.M. Monday through Thursday over a two-week period.

Responses were entered into an IBM mainframe computer and analyzed using SAS (Statistical Analysis System). Tables S1-10 through S1-17 summarize the results.

Findings

Table S1-10 compares the perceptions of FNB customers to the perceptions of customers of all other banks regarding banks in general.

Table S1-11 shows perceptions of FNB customers compared to perceptions of customers of all other banks for questions specifically about the banks where respondents did business. Please note some of these questions are also found in Table S1-10.

Table S1-12 again compares FNB customers to customers of all other banks regarding their perceptions of why they selected their banks. Three reasons (marked with an asterisk) are statistically significant at a level of p (probability) $< .05$. This means that less than a 5 percent probability exists that differences between the responses were related to chance.

Table S1-13 has index numbers that reveal the relative importance of the items in Table S1-12. The higher the index number, the more important the item is perceived to be. Table S1-14 presents customer-perceived quality of services offered by banks. Table S1-15 indexes perceptions contained in Table S1-14.

Table S1-16 shows the frequency of use of services offered by FNB and all other banks respectively. Table S1-17 ranks the services used by an index number. As you might expect, checking account use was most frequently used; estate planning was least used.

With that final table, the ProCom researchers have turned over to you all the data amassed. Now you must spend some time pondering the meaning of it all and its potential uses.

Bank Officers

FNB has several officers, but four are especially important. Olan D. Gable is president and chief executive officer, a role he inherited from his father, who inherited it from his father. Gable has been active in the leadership of the state bankers' association, having just finished his second term as president. Gable got his management degree at State University several years ago. He's recognized by peers as a "banker's banker." He travels a good bit to conduct training workshops and seminars for both the state and national associations.

Samuel A. Penny is the comptroller and vice president of operations. Penny dropped out of the finance program during his junior year at State University to serve in the Viet Nam War. He became a career officer and had four assignments at the Office of Management and Budget in Washington before he retired to join FNB last year.

Phillip P. Bucks is vice president and senior loan officer. Bucks was orphaned at seven when his parents were killed in an automobile crash. He was raised by his maternal grandmother, who provided him with a small fixed income. Bucks worked odd jobs during his public school years and put himself through the finance and marketing programs at state university on grants, loans and scholarships. At 35, he's regarded by insiders as the officer most likely to succeed Gable when he retires seven years from now. Although Gable has two daughters, neither is interested in operating the bank and both live out of state.

Gladys Tidings is vice president in charge of customer relations and communications. She has many good ideas, but Gable and the board resist change, which makes it hard to get her plans approved and implemented. Sometimes she thinks that Gable, especially, and the board fight her recommendations simply because she's female. But in her three years at FNB, she's won their support more often than not.

Board of Directors

Gable also is chairman of the six-member FNB board of directors. Stock in FNB is all privately held, with Gable owning a 56 percent share. I. Nugent Vestor owns 12 percent. Vestor manages his own investments in several local and statewide companies. Tarry L. Onger owns 10 percent. Onger has extensive farm holdings in the Serene area. He and Vestor don't get along well and each has tried repeatedly to buy the other's interest in FNB. Harry D. Ware owns 8 percent of FNB. He heads HDW, with corporate headquarters in Serene, a chain of 21 hardware and building supply stores in the state.

O. T. House owns 10 percent of FNB. Mary I. Factor owns 4 percent of FNB's stock. She's really not much interested in the bank, preferring to focus on running her MIF cosmetics and beauty supply company that serves markets in 11 states. She's on the board at Gable's request (they were college classmates) because she's a peacemaker who can smooth the waters when Onger and Vestor go after each other.

Personal Notes about FNB -

Table S1-1: Total Time Deposits in Serene Banks * (000), Period Ending December 31

Year	FNB	%Tot	SNB	%Tot	FSB	%Tot	FAB	%Tot	ENB	%Tot	CSB	%Tot	Total	%G	Cum %G
1970	4,364	32	4,165	30	5,172	38	----		----		----		13,683	----	----
1975	7,482	25	7,166	24	10,044	33	3,838	13	1,593	5	----		30,123	120	120
1980	21,377	25	14,172	16	28,317	33	12,508	14	10,549	12	----		86,923	189	535
1985	34,522	21	26,279	16	57,450	36	32,907	20	10,065	6	----		162,223	87	1,173
1986	43,818	20	31,373	14	88,938	41	42,300	19	10,813	5	1,233	1	218,475	35	1,497
1987	47,815	16	57,055	20	107,566	37	56,481	19	13,486	5	7,447	2	289,832	33	2,018
1988	63,877	16	67,080	17	148,343	38	79,461	20	17,225	5	15,382	4	391,368	35	2,760
1989	78,588	16	65,921	14	182,124	38	97,877	13	25,101	5	30,993	6	480,604	23	3,412
1990	96,154	18	99,907	18	192,301	34	108,691	19	31,930	6	36,839	7	565,822	18	4,035
1991	104,729	19	108,625	20	194,303	35	105,932	19	38,432	7	**		552,021	2	4,034

* Derived from bank calls. ** Not in last call. Distorts final figures. Some percentages may not add to 100 because of rounding.

Table S1-2: Total Demand Deposits in Serene Banks * (000), Period Ending December 31

Year	FNB	%Tot	SNB	%Tot	FSB	%Tot	FAB	%Tot	ENB	%Tot	CSB	%Tot	Total	%G	Cum %G
1970	3,898	24	5,796	36	6,593	40	----		----		----		16,287	----	----
1975	5,212	22	5,798	24	8,422	35	3,094	13	1,341	6	----		23,867	65	65
1980	9,199	20	10,058	21	16,129	32	7,125	15	4,305	9	----		46,816	96	187
1985	15,934	16	13,223	16	30,207	37	17,158	21	5,361	7	----		81,883	75	403
1986	18,322	19	13,454	14	38,497	39	20,272	21	6,239	7	1,247	1	98,031	20	502
1987	21,482	19	19,260	17	41,295	36	23,070	20	6,149	5	4,362	4	115,618	18	610
1988	15,643	13	16,674	14	50,891	42	26,722	22	6,281	5	6,396	5	122,607	6	653
1989	15,539	15	15,074	15	36,808	36	21,694	21	6,924	7	7,287	7	103,331	-2	534
1990	16,760	15	15,868	14	37,598	34	20,084	18	5,903	5	15,162	14	111,375	10	584
1991	14,358	16	15,503	17	37,357	41	19,137	21	5,397	6	**		91,752	-7	563

* Derived from bank calls. ** Not in last call. Distorts final figures. Some percentages may not add to 100 because of rounding.

Table S1-3: Total Deposits in Serene Banks * (000), Period Ending December 31

Year	FNB	%Tot	SNB	%Tot	FSB	%Tot	FAB	%Tot	ENB	%Tot	CSB	%Tot	Total	%G	Cum % G
1970	8,244	27	9,961	33	11,765	40	---		---		---		28,970	---	---
1975	12,694	24	12,964	25	18,466	34	6,932	13	2,934	5	---		53,990	86	86
1980	21,377	23	24,230	18	44,446	33	19,634	15	14,853	11	---		133,739	148	362
1985	30,576	21	39,502	16	88,657	36	50,065	21	15,426	6	---		244,106	83	742
1986	62,140	20	44,827	14	127,435	40	62,572	20	17,052	5	2,480	1	316,506	30	993
1987	69,297	17	70,015	18	148,861	37	79,551	20	19,617	5	11,809	3	399,150	26	1,078
1988	79,520	15	93,754	16	199,234	39	106,183	21	23,506	5	21,778	4	513,975	29	1,674
1989	94,127	16	81,000	19	219,722	38	119,571	20	32,025	5	38,280	7	584,725	14	1,918
1990	112,914	17	115,775	17	229,899	34	128,775	19	37,833	6	52,001	8	677,197	16	2,238
1991	119,113	17	124,128	18	231,660	33	125,069	18	43,830	6	61,882	9	705,682	4	2,336

* Derived from bank calls. Some percentages may not add to 100 because of rounding.

Table S1-4: Total Assets in Serene Banks * (000), Period Ending December 31

Year	FNB	%Tot	SNB	%Tot	FSB	%Tot	FAB	%Tot	ENB	%Tot	CSB	%Tot	Total	%G	Cum % G
1970	13,124	28.7	15,473	33.8	17,139	37.5	---		---		---		45,736	---	---
1975	19,689	24.3	17,117	21.2	25,708	31.8	10,708	13.3	7,630	9.4	---		80,899	76.9	76.9
1980	34,535	22.9	27,380	18.2	48,909	32.5	22,202	14.8	17,460	11.6	---		150,487	86.0	229.0
1985	56,665	20.2	51,277	18.3	100,071	35.8	54,545	18.5	17,303	6.2	---		279,861	85.9	511.9
1986	69,550	19.3	60,005	16.7	138,977	38.6	68,053	18.9	18,984	5.3	4,081	1.1	359,650	28.5	686.4
1987	77,989	17.7	77,540	17.6	163,464	37.0	86,412	19.6	22,239	5	13,684	3.1	441,328	22.7	864.9
1988	90,189	15.6	97,540	16.9	218,861	37.4	117,402	20.3	27,483	4.6	26,684	4.6	577,852	30.9	1163.5
1989	106,423	15.7	114,419	16.9	249,862	36.8	131,113	19.3	35,696	3.8	41,778	6.2	679,291	17.6	1385.5
1990	125,474	16.7	129,312	17.2	255,515	34.0	140,669	18.7	41,787	5.6	58,040	7.7	750,797	10.5	1540.6
1991	133,451	17.3	134,118	17.4	252,911	32.8	137,106	17.8	47,713	6.2	66,503	8.6	771,802	10.3	1587.5

* Derived from bank calls. Some percentages may not add to 100 because of rounding.

Table S1-5: Index of Serene Banks,* Period Ending December 31

Year	FNB	SNB	FSB	FAB	ENB	CSB	Combined
1970	12	14	7	—	—	—	7
1975	18	15	10	8	21	—	12
1980	32	30	20	17	49	—	22
1985	53	49	40	42	48	—	41
1986	65	52	57	52	53	10	53
1987	73	68	65	66	62	33	65
1988	85	85	86	90	77	63	85
1989	100	100	100	100	100	100	100
1990	119	113	102	107	117	138	111
1991	125	117	101	105	134	159	114

*Derived from bank calls. **Base year is 100% of total assets of each bank.

Table S1-6: Total Loans by Serene Banks * (000), Period Ending December 31

Year	FNB	%Tot	SNB	%Tot	FSB	%Tot	FAB	%Tot	ENB	%Tot	CSB	%Tot	Total	%G	Cum % G
1,970	5,636	30	5,713	30	7,816	40	—		—		—		19,165	—	—
1,975	8,914	23	9,590	24	13,365	34	5,085	13	2,405	6	—		39,359	105	105
1,980	17,749	22	14,468	18	27,828	34	11,860	15	8,848	11	—		80,753	105	321
1,985	29,235	19	24,320	16	28,508	36	32,907	21	10,986	7	—		155,956	75	713
1,986	34,402	17	31,660	16	77,416	39	41,362	21	12,265	6	541	1	197,557	21	931
1,987	41,462	16	44,077	17	97,707	38	50,445	19	14,742	6	8,041	6	256,391	30	1,238
1,988	48,806	10	58,580	12	130,725	27	76,126	16	19,950	4	15,263	3	489,760	23	2,455
1,989	63,382	14	67,229	15	167,748	38	84,251	19	26,718	6	29,815	7	439,043	-1	2,191
1,990	68,215	15	69,238	15	167,443	36	90,728	19	31,991	7	38,630	8	466,245	6	2,332
1,991	70,421	14	76,994	16	183,106	37	85,057	17	34,432	7	43,374	9	493,384	6	2,474

* Derived from bank calls. Some percentages may not add to 100 because of rounding.

Table S1-7: Total Capital of Serene Banks * (000), Periods ending December 31

Year	FNB	%Tot	SNB	%Tot	FSB	%Tot	FAB	%Tot	ENB	%Tot	CSB	%Tot	Total	%G	Cum % G
1970	1,090	31	1,011	29	1,379	40	---		---		---		3,480	---	---
1975	1,349	22	1,334	22	1,887	31	960	16	590	9	---		6,120	76	86
1980	2,818	24	2,231	19	3,646	36	1,837	16	1,040	9	---		11,572	89	362
1985	5,382	27	3,447	17	6,597	33	3,064	15	1,463	7	---		19,953	72	742
1986	6,104	24	4,186	17	8,196	32	3,773	15	1,443	6	1,548	6	25,250	27	993
1987	6,977	23	6,147	20	9,965	32	4,610	15	1,550	5	1,689	6	30,938	11	1,078
1988	7,996	21	7,290	19	13,137	34	6,044	16	1,734	5	2,046	5	38,250	24	1,674
1989	9,417	20	8,353	19	16,247	35	7,647	17	2,150	5	2,530	6	46,344	21	1,918
1990	11,059	21	8,461	16	17,190	33	9,585	18	2,224	4	3,730	7	52,359	13	2,238
1991	11,882	24	6,242	13	15,254	31	9,630	20	3,221	7	3,271	7	49,500	-6	2,336

* Derived from bank calls. Some percentages may not add to 100 because of rounding.

Table S1-8: Serene Bank Capital-to-Loan Ratios,* Period Ending December 31

Year	FNB	SNB	FSB	FAB	ENB	CSB	Mean
1970	1:8.2	1:5.7	1:6.7	---	---	---	1:6.9
1975	1:6.6	1:7.2	1:7.1	1:5.3	1:4.1	---	1:6.1
1980	1:6.3	1:6.5	1:7.6	1:6.5	1:8.5	---	1:7.1
1985	1:5.4	1:7.0	1:8.7	1:10.7	1:7.5	---	1:7.9
1986	1:5.6	1:7.6	1:9.4	1:11.0	1:8.5	1:0.3	1:7.1
1987	1:5.9	1:7.2	1:9.8	1:10.9	1:9.5	1:4.8	1:8.1
1988	1:6.1	1:8.0	1:9.6	1:12.6	1:11.5	1:7.4	1:9.2
1989	1:6.7	1:8.0	1:10.3	1:11.0	1:12.4	1:11.8	1:10.0
1990	1:6.2	1:8.9	1:9.7	1:9.5	1:13.7	1:10.4	1:9.7
1991	1:6.9	1:12.3	1:12.0	1:8.8	1:10.7	1:13.3	1:9.7

* Ratios calculated from bank calls.

Table S1-9: Serene Banks Compared on Key Dimensions in 1991 (000)

	FNB	SNB	FSB	FAB	ENB	CSB
Total Assets	133,451	134,118	252,911	137,106	47,713	66,503
Equity Capital	11,882	6,242	15,254	9,630	3,221	3,271
Total Deposits	119,113	124,128	231,660	125,069	43,830	61,882
Equity-to-Liabilities	10	5	6.6	7.7	7.3	5.3
Loans	70,421	46,994	183,106	85,057	34,432	43,374
Equity-to-Assets	8.9	4.7	6	7	6.8	4.9
Loans-to-deposits	59.1	62	79	68	78.6	70.1
Loans-to-Capital	5.9	12.3	12	8.8	10.7	13.3
Time Deposits	104,729	108,625	194,303	105,932	38,432	**
Demand Deposits	14,384	15,503	37,357	19,137	5,397	**

** Not included in final bank call of 1991.

Table S1-10: Perceptions of Banks in General

Attitudes	Customers of FNB					Customers of Other Banks				
	*SA	A	N	D	SDA	SA	A	N	D	SDA
Banks today are more financially secure than they were five years ago.	6.2	40.0	15.5	37.7	4.4	2.8	33.9	18.4	40.7	3.9
Banks today are more cautious about lending money than they were five years ago.	8.8	66.6	11.1	11.1	2.2	18.1	53.2	15.5	12.1	0.8
Banks today have a better record of guarding deposits than they had five years ago.	6.6	37.7	40.0	13.3	2.2	3.4	43.9	31.1	19.8	1.7
I have more confidence in banks than I did five years ago.	6.6	28.8	13.3	48.8	2.2	2.2	32.5	21.8	36.8	6.5
I am less concerned today with the safety of deposits in banks than I was five years ago.	4.4	44.4	20.0	31.1	-	2.8	32.6	18.7	41.7	3.9
I believe banks today are more financially stable than they were five years ago.	6.6	24.4	13.3	51.1	4.4	1.4	26.9	14.4	54.2	2.8
Laws and regulations are more adequate today to protect depositors than they were five years ago.	6.5	46.6	28.6	20.8	-	2.5	45.3	32.0	18.4	1.7
The general public has more confidence in banks today than it had five years ago.	4.4	26.8	8.8	51.1	8.8	1.7	18.7	13.3	59.3	6.8
It is more important for people to know personally their bankers than it was five years ago.	11.1	71.1	11.1	6.7	-	13.8	55.2	15.0	15.8	-

* SA = Strongly Agree; A = Agree; N = Neither; D = Disagree; SDA = Strongly Disagree. Some percentages may not add to 100 because of rounding.

Table S1-11: Perceptions of Their Own Banks

Attitudes	Customers of FNB					Customers of Other Banks				
	*SA	A	N	D	SDA	SA	A	N	D	SDA
My bank is more financially secure than it was five years ago.	6.6	35.5	44.4	13.3	-	5.1	37.6	47.5	9.0	0.5
My bank is more cautious today about lending money than it was five years ago.	8.9	44.4	42.2	4.4	-	9.9	44.7	39.0	6.2	-
My bank has a better record of guarding deposits than it had five years ago.	6.6	46.6	46.6	-	-	4.8	36.9	53.6	4.5	-
I have more confidence in my bank today than I had five years ago.	6.6	40.0	46.6	6.7	-	3.9	36.2	42.7	16.4	0.5
I am less concerned today with the safety of deposits in my bank than five years ago.	6.6	42.2	40.0	11.1	-	3.4	28.3	39.9	26.0	2.2
I believe my bank is more financial stable than it was five years ago.	4.4	40.0	48.8	6.6	-	5.1	36.8	48.1	8.5	1.4
It is more important for me to know personally my bankers today than it was five years ago.	8.8	44.4	28.8	17.7	-	11.6	42.4	30.0	15.3	0.5

* SA = Agree; A = Agree; N = Neither; D = Disagree; SDA = Strongly disagree. Some perecentages may not add to 100 because of rounding.

Table S1-12: Frequency of Reasons Why Customers Selected Their Banks

Reasons	FNB				All Other Banks			
	*VI	I	SI	U	VI	I	SI	U
Ease of getting to the bank from home.	17.7	44.4	17.7	20.0	25.5	43.6	15.0	15.8
Ease of getting to the bank from work.	13.3	35.5	15.5	35.5	14.7	31.4	18.1	35.6
Interest rates on regular savings accounts.	17.7	53.3	8.8	20.0	15.0	40.2	13.0	31.7
Interest rates on checking accounts.	17.7	51.1	4.4	26.6	15.3	36.5	11.3	36.8
Interest rates on certificates of deposits and money markets.	24.4	40.0	2.2	33.3	22.6	36.2	7.0	33.9
Interest rates on personal loans.	28.8	42.2	6.6	46.6	15.3	23.2	8.2	53.2
Conveneience of banking hours. **	48.8	24.4	8.8	17.7	40.2	45.3	7.3	7.0
Convenience of branch banking.	13.3	22.2	6.6	57.7	20.1	33.1	10.2	36.5
Convenience of ATMs. **	24.2	24.2	-	51.1	26.6	28.3	11.3	33.7
Convenience of drive-in tellers.	37.7	40.0	8.8	13.3	33.9	43.6	11.6	10.7
Convenience of 24-hour depository.	17.7	24.4	15.5	42.2	15.0	30.5	15.0	39.3
Quality of financial counselling and guidance. **	8.8	51.1	4.4	35.5	17.2	36.2	16.1	30.3
Financial strength of the bank.	51.1	44.4	2.2	2.2	47.3	42.2	5.9	4.5
Willingness to consider my financial needs fairly.	24.4	68.8	4.4	2.2	37.3	47.8	7.6	7.0
Monthly statements from my bank are easy to understand.	55.5	40.0	2.2	2.2	47.5	44.1	5.6	2.5
Personally acquainted with an officer at the bank.	15.5	44.4	2.2	37.3	16.4	32.5	15.5	35.4
Personally acquainted with other bank personnel.	11.1	28.8	11.1	48.8	7.6	27.7	20.9	43.6
Variety of services at the bank.	20.0	64.4	4.4	11.1	23.2	52.6	17.2	6.8
Professional handling of loan applications.	20.0	51.2	4.4	24.4	28.0	43.9	8.5	19.5
Safety of my deposits at this bank.	66.6	28.8	-	4.4	55.8	37.1	4.5	2.5
Trustworthiness of bank officers.	64.4	35.5	-	-	57.1	34.9	4.5	3.4

* VI = Very Important; I = Important; SI = Somewhat Important; U = Unimportant Some perecentages may not add to 100 because of rounding. ** Difference is statistically significant at p < .05.

Table S1-13: Index of Reasons Why Customers Selected Their Banks

Reasons	FNB	Other Banks
Trustworthiness of bank officers.	364	345
Safety of my deposits at this bank.	357	346
Monthly statements from my bank are easy to understand.	348	336
Financial strength of this bank.	315	332
Willingness to consider my financial needs fairly.	315	315
Convenience of banking hours.	304	318
Convenience of drive-in tellers.	302	300
Variety of services at this bank.	293	292
Interest rates on personal loans.	273	259
Interest rates on regular savings account.	268	238
Professional handling of loan applications.	266	280
Interest rates on checking accounts.	260	240
Interest rates on certificates of deposits and money markets.	255	247
Personally acquainted with a bank officer.	237	230
Quality of financial counselling and guidance.	233	240
Ease of getting to bank from work.	226	225
Convenience of ATMs.	222	247
Convenience of 24-hour depository.	217	221
Interest rates on commercial or business loans.	208	200
Personally acquainted with some bank personnel.	202	199
Convenience of branch banking.	191	236

Table S1-15: Index of Perceived Quality of Services Rendered by Banks

Reasons	FNB	Other Banks
Pleasantness of atmosphere at my bank.	431	407
Efficiency of taking care of my banking needs.	424	390
Reliable and accurate handling of my banking transactions.	420	391
Knowledgeable handling of my financial needs.	402	364
Fairness of bank policies.	397	357
Adequacy of information on loans and interest.	380	350
Ease of discussing financial needs with an officer.	371	346
Interest or dividends paid on deposits or investments.	360	344
Professional handling of loan applications.	357	342
Availability of a loan officer.	353	343
Ease of applying for a personal loan.	351	343

Table S1-14: Perceptions of the Quality of Services Rendered by Banks

Types of Service	FNB					All Other Banks				
	*S	VG	A	BA	P	S	VG	A	BA	P
Ease of discussing financial needs with an officer.	22.2	26.6	51.1	-	-	12.1	28.6	55.2	1.4	2.5
Availability of a loan officers.	17.7	24.4	53.3	-	-	9.7	30.8	56.3	1.7	1.9
Adequacy of information on loans and interest.	22.2	37.7	37.7	2.2	-	9.3	36.5	50.9	1.3	1.9
Interest or dividends paid on deposits/investments	17.7	24.4	57.7	-	-	9.0	30.0	58.3	1.7	0.9
Fairness of bank policies. **	31.1	35.5	33.3	-	-	9.6	43.6	42.4	2.8	1.4
Efficiency of taking care of my banking needs. **	48.0	48.8	6.6	4.4	-	22.0	50.7	23.5	2.5	1.1
Pleasantness of the atmosphere at the bank.	46.6	37.7	15.5	-	-	29.1	51.5	16.7	2.2	0.2
Ease of applying for a personal loan.	13.3	31.1	51.1	2.2	-	9.4	24.5	62.9	1.7	1.4
Knowledgeable handling of my financial needs.	26.6	48.8	24.4	-	-	13.3	43.1	39.7	2.7	1.4
Reliable and accurate handling of banking transactions.	37.7	46.6	13.3	2.2	-	23.2	50.7	21.8	2.5	1.7
Professional handling of loan applications.	17.7	26.6	51.1	4.4	-	9.3	27.2	60.9	1.4	1.1

* S = Superior; VG = Very Good; A = Average; BA = Below Average; P = Poor. Some percentages may not add to 100 because of rounding.

** Difference is statistically significant at $p < .05$.

Table S1-16: Frequency of Use of Services Rendered by Banks

Services	FNB								All Other Banks							
	*D	W	2M	M	2Y	1Y	E	N	D	W	2M	M	2Y	1Y	E	N
Regular checking account.	55.5	24.4	11.1	4.4	-	-	-	4.4	52.1	34.6	5.6	3.9	-	-	1.7	1.7
Commercial or business checking account.	4.4	13.3	2.2	-	-	2.2	2.2	75.5	9.9	5.6	0.8	2.2	0.5	0.5	1.9	78.1
Checking account with interest.	17.7	4.4	6.6	6.6	2.2	-	2.2	60.0	7.6	7.9	2.8	7.9	1.7	1.1	3.4	67.4
Certificate of deposit account.	4.5	4.5	-	9.0	2.2	9.9	2.2	68.1	0.5	0.8	0.2	5.1	3.9	13.8	5.9	69.4
Money market checking account.	2.2	2.2	-	4.4	-	-	2.2	88.8	0.8	1.1	0.5	4.2	1.4	3.6	2.5	85.5
Passbook savings account.	-	-	4.0	13.3	4.4	4.4	6.6	66.6	1.1	4.5	3.6	15.5	8.5	6.8	7.0	52.6
Money market savings account.	-	2.2	-	2.2	2.2	4.4	-	88.8	0.2	0.5	0.5	5.1	1.9	3.9	2.2	85.2
Automobile loan.	-	-	-	16.6	-	5.2	11.2	56.7	0.2	0.2	5.6	-	0.2	5.1	15.5	72.8
Home improvement loan.	-	-	2.2	-	-	2.2	2.2	93.3	-	-	0.5	-	0.2	1.1	5.1	92.9
Personal loan.	-	-	-	-	-	13.3	11.1	75.5	0.2	-	0.5	5.1	1.9	7.6	9.0	75.3
Business loan.	-	-	-	-	4.4	-	4.4	91.1	-	-	0.2	1.9	1.9	3.4	5.1	87.2
Construction loan.	-	-	-	-	-	-	-	97.7	0.2	-	-	0.8	1.3	1.1	2.8	93.7
Estate planning services.	-	-	-	-	-	2.2	2.2	97.7	-	-	-	0.2	0.2	1.7	1.9	96.3
Personal trust services.	2.2	-	-	2.2	2.2	2.2	-	91.1	1.4	-	1.1	0.8	0.2	1.7	1.9	92.6
Drive-in tellers.	11.1	28.8	28.8	15.5	4.4	2.2	2.2	6.6	7.6	48.0	12.2	13.6	5.4	1.9	1.4	9.6
Automatic teller machines.	2.2	17.7	6.6	2.2	4.4	-	4.4	62.2	8.5	26.4	7.1	9.6	3.4	1.4	1.9	40.9
Buy or sell stocks or options.	-	-	-	-	-	2.2	-	97.8	0.2	0.8	0.2	0.2	0.2	0.5	2.2	96.1
Buy or sell government or muni bonds. **	-	-	-	-	2.2	6.6	2.2	88.8	-	-	-	0.8	0.2	0.8	1.9	96.0
IRA or KEOGH retirement account.	-	-	-	-	2.2	2.2	2.2	95.5	-	-	0.2	1.1	0.5	7.3	1.9	88.6
VISA or MC account.	2.2	4.4	2.2	11.1	-	8.8	2.2	68.8	1.1	4.5	2.2	7.6	1.7	1.7	2.8	78.1
Cashier's checks or money orders.	-	2.2	6.6	6.6	2.2	26.6	17.7	37.7	0.2	0.8	3.4	7.0	12.1	25.5	10.2	40.5
Traveler's checks.	-	-	-	-	13.3	24.4	13.3	48.8	0.2	-	0.2	1.1	6.2	30.8	9.9	51.2
U.S. savings bonds. **	-	2.2	2.2	-	4.4	2.2	2.2	86.6	-	-	-	0.5	0.2	1.9	3.4	93.7
Foreign currency exchange.	-	-	-	-	2.2	4.4	4.4	88.8	-	-	-	0.2	0.2	4.2	4.8	90.3
Direct deposit.	-	6.6	13.3	17.7	-	-	4.4	57.7	0.2	7.9	11.3	16.7	1.4	0.8	3.1	58.3
Night depository.	-	-	11.1	13.3	5.5	2.5	7.6	11.3	1.7	2.87	4.5	7.3	4.8	4.2	3.4	71.1
Safety deposit box.	2.2	-	-	2.2	8.8	13.3	2.2	71.1	-	0.8	0.8	5.6	5.6	8.5	1.7	76.4
Financial planning and counseling.	-	-	-	-	2.2	4.4	6.6	86.6	-	-	-	0.8	3.4	9.6	3.9	82.1

* D = Daily; W = Weekly; 2M = Twice Monthly; M = Monthly; 2Y = Twice Yearly; Y = Yearly; E = Ever; N = Never. Some pereentages may not add to 100 because of roiunding.

** Difference is statistically significant at $p < .05$.

Table S1-17: Index of Frequency of Use of Services Rendered by Banks

Services	FNB	Other Banks
Regular checking account.	701	719
Drive-in tellers.	577	578
Checking account with interest.	320	257
Direct deposit.	282	282
Automatic teller machines.	282	409
Cashier's checks or money orders.	251	250
Commercial or business checking.	228	221
Certificate of deposit account.	222	176
Visa of MasterCard account.	217	188
Passbook savings.	204	262
Travelers checks.	202	198
Night depository.	188	207
Safety deposit.	180	169
Automobile loan.	155	152
Money market checking account.	148	146
U.S. savings bonds.	140	110
Personal loan.	137	155
Money market savings.	137	144
Personal trust service.	133	123
Financial counseling and planning.	122	136
Buy or sell government or municipal bonds.	122	107
Foreign currency exchange.	120	115
Business loan.	117	127
Home improvement loan.	115	110
Buy or sell stocks or options.	108	113
IRA or KEOGH.	106	124
Construction loan.	104	113
Estate planning.	102	106

Scenario 2 — National Association of Trauma Specialists

The National Association of Trauma Specialists (NATS) was organized in 1956 in Chicago by doctors specializing in emergency medicine. It is an association of practicing and retired physicians who elected to specialize in the study and treatment of trauma as the primary cause of deaths among people injured in accidents of all types.

History

Studies of casualty statistics from World War II suggested that about 65 percent of the deaths from battlefield wounds resulted more from the trauma induced by the wounds than by the wounds themselves. Trauma can be described generally as a shock to the human body induced by any external agent. That statistic led medical researchers to theorize that rapid treatment to stabilize traumatized soldiers would increase time for effective treatment of the wounds themselves.

The theory was put into practice during the Korean War (although some people still prefer to call that war a police action). Mobile Army Surgical Hospitals (MASH, as in the movie and television series of the same name) were set up close to the front lines. Helicopters carried the wounded quickly to these field hospitals. Although some repair and treatment of wounds was done by MASH units, their primary purpose was to treat the trauma and stabilize wounded soldiers as quickly as possible. Wounded were then taken to regular hospitals for appropriate treatment, surgical reconstruction or other therapeutic procedures.

The concept proved so successful in reducing battlefield deaths that after the war some surgeons adapted the method to civilian practice. It wasn't long before medical students began preparing for careers in the practice of emergency medicine. This produced a small stream of new physicians especially trained to treat major injuries, such as those that occur in automobile accidents. Each year a staggering number of deaths is caused by accidents in the United States. The practice of emergency medicine has mushroomed.

The Association

More than 12,000 physicians and other medical personnel were members of NATS at the end of last year. They are mostly from the United States, but 18 percent of them are from 22 foreign countries. Because of the high cost of equipping and staffing a complete trauma treatment unit, most emergency rooms staffed with trauma specialists are found only in major hospitals.

Doctors specializing in emergency medicine must complete a specialty residency following completion of their medical studies. The association offers continuing education programs to doctors and other personnel. These programs are often presented at various medical schools or teaching hospitals, with sessions usually lasting from two to five days each. The annual NATS convention also offers technical training sessions as well as medical papers that explain the latest research findings in trauma diagnosis and treatment.

NATS Communication Program

The NATS communication program includes a monthly newsletter, *Traumatic*. It features research findings in brief, the association's lobbying efforts at the state and national levels and interpretations of and opinions about proposed legislation that might affect emergency care. Technical bulletins, known as *Traumatech*, are distributed irregularly during the year to the membership. The number of bulletins has ranged annually from 9 to 27 during the last five years.

A quarterly four-color journal, *Emergency Medicine*, circulates not only to NATS members but also to other members of the American Medical Association (AMA) and hospital administrators. The editorial thrust emphasizes the positive aspects of emergency medicine and the need to expand facilities and staff.

NATS Problems

For two primary reasons, morale among NATS members is poor and falling.

First, emergency room physicians work a 70-hour week, on the average. This is not only physically demanding and debilitating, it also takes them away from their families, resulting in higher rates of divorce, alcohol and drug abuse than in any other segment of the medical community.

Second, the demand on most major emergency rooms is about 133 percent beyond planned capacity. Thus, if you walk through a major emergency room, you'll probably find patients in hallways and lounges waiting for treatment because treatment rooms are full.

Membership Survey

A recent survey shows that 71.5 percent of the NATS membership sees the combination of hours and work load as untenable. An internal analysis of membership trends, completed Tuesday of last week, shows the association, starting two years ago, began to lose 20 members for each 19 it gained. This analysis has neither been reported to the association, although that is expected to happen soon, nor has it been shared with the public.

One of the most disturbing statistics related to emergency room medicine is that about 60 percent of those treated are involved in preventable accidents. Approximately 30 percent of these preventable accidents are auto accidents involving alcohol or drug abuse.

Furthermore, about 25 percent of those who seek emergency treatment aren't emergencies at all. Stomachaches, headaches, sore muscles and nonemergency conditions like minor cuts should wait to be treated by the patients' own physicians.

Emergency Room Overload

The NATS leadership believes much of the emergency room overload is attributable to these nonemergency cases because the public is not educated about the legitimate uses and purposes of emergency room medicine. Cases abound where accident victims have died or nearly died unnecessarily because emergency room facilities were clogged by people seeking treatment for minor cuts, scrapes and diarrhea.

Serene and NATS

NATS was founded and headquartered in Chicago until seven years ago when it moved to Serene. The board of directors, in concert with the association's executive team, recommended to the membership, which approved it overwhelmingly by mail ballot, to move to Serene for five major reasons:

1. The State University has a large medical complex in Serene.

2. Two members of the university's acclaimed medical faculty won back-to-back Nobel Prizes in Medicine. Both are emergency medicine specialists.

3. The state medical school is generally recognized as being on the leading edge of emergency room diagnosis and treatment, research and practices.

4. A good transportation system makes it easy for even international visitors, and there are many of them, to travel to and from Serene.

5. Serene is in a semi-pastoral setting that appeals to middle- and upper-income families and there is no town-and-gown split in the community.

Major NATS Players

The executive staff of NATS is headed by H. Arthur (Arty) Hart, who has served as executive director for 10 years His medical degree and emergency room studies focused on thoracic medicine (the chest cavity). Barry P. Tallant, director of operations, is not a physician but has an MBA degree from State University in operations management. Many of the NATS staff see him as a buttoned-down, three-piece pinstriper who won't be at NATS much longer because he's ambitious to run his own organization.

The director of financial affairs is Patricia (Patsy) R. Bills. She has advanced degrees in nursing and worked six years in a major hospital emergency room before joining NATS three years ago. She joined NATS so she could use her certified public accountancy training to its benefit.

The director of communication is Sally S. Forth, a post she entered just two months ago. Her BA and MA degrees from State University are in public relations. She's spent the last three years as research director at a major agency in New York City. Before that she handled account services in Dallas and Atlanta for six years and was in creative services three years for a major firm in San Francisco. Ms. Forth has a staff of four, plus two interns from State University.

Board of Directors

The six members of the NATS board of directors are elected to two-year staggered terms by secret ballot at the annual convention by members present and voting. The board elects its own chair. Hart Z. Smart, MD, from Kansas City, Missouri is the current chair. Other members are Harry O. Leggs, MD, Lincoln, Nebraska; Walter F. Armes, MD, Corpus Christi, Texas; Brooke N. Bonze, MD, Syracuse, New York; Turner R. Head, MD, San Diego, California and Tyre D. Blood, MD, Denver, Colorado. The immediate past president also sits on the board in an advisory capacity. She is Sterling S. Goodheart, MD, Alexandria, Virginia.

Personal Notes about NATS –

Scenario 3 — National Child-Care Centers

National Child-Care Centers (NCCC) was founded in 1969 to provide quality day-care and child development programs to children from 2 to 12 years old. NCCC was founded by William (Will) Diaperchange and his wife, Needa. But in 1983 they sold NCCC to a holding company that has subsidiaries in the fields of nursing homes (geriatric care), institutional food processing and preparation, catering and others. The formal name of the holding company is Bottoms, Armes, Betters and Yema, Inc., but it goes by the acronym BABY. BABY is traded over the counter (NASDAQ symbol: BABI). The Diaperchanges no longer participate in the management of NCCC except as members of BABY's board of directors.

Beginning Philosophy

The Diaperchanges founded and operated NCCC on one guiding principle: to integrate educational and developmental training with traditional day-care services.

Perhaps it is an unfair characterization, but at that time day care centers were little more than holding pens for the children of working parents.

Although toys abounded and some planned activities were included in most day-care operations, few centers even attempted to integrate childhood developmental programs into their operations. Three primary reasons account for this initially haphazard approach:

1. Center operators believed parents were unwilling or unable to pay the higher costs of such programs.

2. There was a shortage of properly trained personnel whom centers could hire at modest salaries.

3. Most physical facilities were inadequate to the demands of this educational approach.

Most people in the child-care business then thought that the falling birthrate of the 1960s and 1970s signaled a declining market for day-care centers for years to come. They also thought existing private caregivers could easily absorb the number of children entering the day-care market. In general, operators concluded that the demand for full-scale child development and day-care centers was economically unsound and would not attract attention from major investors.

A Different Perspective

The Diaperchanges thought differently. They agreed that the market was only a small percentage of the total number of children needing day-care. But they also believed that small percentage of the children of the 1970s and 1980s would belong mostly to parents reared in the 1960s and 1970s, who, research suggested, valued the quality of life and the opportunities for advancement for their own children. Will and Needa saw these parents and their progeny as part and parcel of the "me generation," as these people were referred to by social commentators.

They further thought enough of these parents would not only want more day-care for their children, but that many would look for caregivers whose skills would speed up their children's social and educational development. And they were willing and could pay for it. Among other interpretations, the Diaperchanges also realized that centers with developmental goals must be conveniently located for these parents. They concluded: These parents are probably willing to pay more for quality care, but they may be equally unwilling, because they don't have the time, to make extended daily side trips to get it.

The Center Is Born

The first Child-Care Center was opened in Dallas, Texas in 1969. It was located on Stemmons Freeway because most forecasts indicated that the areas north and west of downtown Dallas were the most promising for future residential growth. Parents who commute via Stemmons could drop off or pick up their children quickly and easily, thus eliminating time-consuming side trips.

The center was designed with 10 activity rooms, each with a capacity of 10 children. It also included offices for staff, an emergency medical care room, a central assembly hall and a kitchen for preparing and serving hot, nutritious meals. A large portico let parents drive under cover to drop off or pick up their children during bad weather. The grounds were not spacious, but there was ample space for swings, jungle gyms, seesaws, sandboxes and the like.

Because neither Will nor Needa Diaperchange had such training, they hired a specialist in early childhood development. She was named director and was responsible for operating the center and its programs. Although all teachers at the center were not required to hold degrees, the policy was that each supervisor of every age level must have at least one degree and at least three years of professional experience in early childhood development.

Big Business and Child-Care

These early decisions by the Diaperchanges were astute: The first Center quickly filled to capacity. Soon the word *national* was added to form NCCC and by 1983 the NCCC network included 55 centers in Texas, Oklahoma, Louisiana, Kansas and Missouri. By this time, an "echo boom" in the U.S. birthrate had occurred as the children of the so-called baby boom began to reach their 30s.

This "echo boom" resulted in an attractive market opportunity because upwardly mobile young professionals with substantial disposable incomes were at last producing children. Most of these were two-career families.

The child-care market at last had impressive demographics, and psychographics began to attract the interest of big investors looking for profitable opportunities. Several national chains were formed to compete with existing care-givers. Names such as Kindercare, La Petite Academy and Daybridge became prominent.

Enter BABY

BABY, with corporate headquarters in Chicago, became interested. The marketing department at BABY recommended that an existing day-care group be bought. BABY was first rebuffed by Daybridge and then by Kindercare before management decided to go to the founders of the market—NCCC and the Diaperchanges.

Because they had no children and only a few distant relatives with whom they were not close, Will and Needa had talked privately about the need for a succession plan or the possibility of a sale. They were also aware of their ages. Will was then 59 and Needa was 60. Both were in relatively good health.

Negotiators from BABY found willing ears at their first meeting with the Diaperchanges in late January 1983. After several meetings, a deal was struck March 1, 1983, in which $28,000,000 in BABY stock was transferred to Will and Needa, and they became BABY board members for life. The NCCC name was to continue but as a wholly-owned subsidiary of BABY.

Under BABY's ownership, NCCC has grown rapidly and now includes 112 centers in 17 states, none in cities with less than 150,000 population. The original concept of the center and its design have been retained. The only structural change has been, because of growth, to organize NCCC operations into districts with a maximum of 10 centers in each. Each district is headed by a supervisor who reports to NCCC corporate headquarters in Dallas.

The Program

The rate for developmental child-care at an NCCC center is $150.00 weekly per child. Each child is assigned to a room with children of the same age and/or level of educational development.

Each room has at least one teacher with degree qualifications in childhood development and enough teacher aides, some of whom are working on degree programs in early childhood development, to maintain a ratio of one adult to every four children.

Ample time is provided for physical growth and developmental activities, but most of each center day is devoted to structured programs that speed and inspire educational, social and skills development. Statistics show a positive relationship between children who attend NCCC centers and their success in formal schooling.

Enrollment periods at NCCC coincide with local public school calendars. Summer programs are also available.

Major NCCC Players

The NCCC president is George P. Schuss. Schuss is a native Californian who came to NCCC two years ago. He holds degrees in operations management and law. In fact, his former law practice in Santa Barbara was noted for cases that involved children and social service agencies. Schuss is generally regarded as a leading authority on laws affecting day-care centers. He's also regarded as an efficient but people-sensitive manager.

Sully T. Trotter is vice president of marketing. "Sully" is short for Sullivan, a maternal family name. She has undergraduate and graduate degrees in advertising and marketing from the University of Illinois, Champaign. She joined the NCCC management team last year after spending the previous six years as director of market planning for Playskool, Inc., maker and distributor of a wide range of educational toys.

Shirley M. Kidd is vice president of program development. She has BA, MA and PhD degrees, all from the University of Kansas, in early childhood development, as well as an MBA in management from Syracuse. She's been with NCCC six years and is credited with innovative programs that have spurred NCCC's recent growth.

Terry Childers is vice president of communications. His BJ in public relations and MJ in advertising are from the University of Texas at Austin. Having served as an account supervisor for a major agency in New York City for four years, he returned to his native Dallas to join NCCC. He had also worked as an account representative in Dallas (two years) and Chicago (two years).

Major BABY Players

BABY's corporate headquarters is Chicago, Illinois. Its chief executive officer is Manford Z. Topper, who has been in this role since BABY was formed by its four principal investors 15 years ago. Topper had several successful years of brand management with Procter and Gamble, then moved to General Foods as vice president in charge of new product and market planning.

He is a lifelong friend and fraternity brother of Paul V. Betters. It was only natural that Betters and the other BABY principals would turn to Topper because of his stellar credentials. They sweetened the deal with Topper at the end of the first two years with 3 percent of BABY's stock. The rest of the stock was equally divided among the four principals until BABY went public three years ago. Topper and the other four still control 72 percent of BABY's stock.

BABY has four principals. Walter F. Armes is a physician from Corpus Christi, Texas, who made his fortune in real estate development. Paul V. Betters is a real estate developer in Chicago, Illinois.

Harry U. Bottoms from Yonkers, New York, has principal holdings in two cruise lines, oil and gas exploration and distribution and food processing. He is also the principal stockholder in one of the nation's leading retail chains.

Juan Villareal Yema, an entrepreneur from Seattle, has large timber holdings and owns wood-processing plants in the Northwest. He is also a major stockholder in Sun Computers, a Silicon Valley company that expects to challenge IBM and Apple in the office computers arena.

Personal Notes about NCCC -

Scenario 4 — Tentative Electronics, Inc.

T entative Electronics, Inc. (TEI), is a leading manufacturer of automatic teller machines (ATMs) that it sells directly to the financial community. A small sales force concentrates on banks, savings and loans, thrifts and credit unions.

TEI designed and installed the first ATM in 1972. It allowed customers with special cards to withdraw cash at sites remote from teller windows. TEI still holds the patent on this primitive machine. With each new electronic advancement, TEI has adapted its products so that it is generally seen by the financial community as an innovative, visionary company.

As TEI thrived, it added other products. Now it has three operating divisions. The financial services division markets a full line of ATMs and related peripherals. A data-processing division markets electronic data-processing services and consulting services.

An office products division markets mini- and microcomputers with software applications used in much of the industry. This division sometimes works extensively with the data-processing division to produce custom software for major clients. TEI's over-the-counter stock uses the NASDAQ symbol TEI.

The Products

TEI's cash cow is the Money Machine 2001. This is a fascia-mounted unit equipped to do a full array of financial transactions. It dispenses cash and debits to credit cards or checking accounts, accepts deposits and payments on installment accounts and reports account summary information such as balances, loan balances, credit card balances, history of transactions and the like.

The Money Machine 2001 is priced at $34,500, including equipment and software, but not installation. Buyers assume the full cost of cutting holes in walls and getting proper coaxial and power cables for installation sites. TEI's installation crew will install the ATM and test its performance for a flat fee of $4,000. Units are guaranteed to work properly for one year when TEI does the installation. Any problems are corrected at TEI's expense. Local vendors can also install and test the units for about $2,500. Local vendor guarantees vary. But when vendors install the units, TEI's guarantee is only for 90 days on hardware and software, plus labor costs. Competitive units are marketed by Docutel, Diebold and Lefebre.

TEI's office products division markets two computer control systems, each with different software. The M1 Financial System is a minicomputer with sophisticated software that supports cash management, management of demand and time deposit accounts, accounts receivable and payable, journal entries and a versatile data base. This system is designed for banks with assets up to about $100,000,000 or branches of larger banking units.

The M10 Financial System is a microprocessor-based system that appeals mostly to branches of savings and loans, credit unions or other small financial units. The M10 offers a full array of account management reports and can handle up to 10,000 separate accounts. In addition, TEI's office products division also markets a wide selection of calculators and accounting machines and related supplies.

TEI's Problems

TEI has a long history of profitability. But recent events have cast shadows on Tentative's future. Many of these events date from the mid-1980s when the number of insolvent banks rose dramatically and exceeded failures recorded during the U.S.'s Great Depression.

Observers seem to think the banking industry has lost most of its bad blood, and some forecasts are even moderately rosy. But some Federal Reserve people say the raw number of banks may drop from about 12,500 to as few as 7,000 before the banking industry stabilizes.

The stock market took its sharpest loss ever in 1989 during the height of the savings and loan debacle, even outstripping the crash of 1929. It has rebounded, but it's been a roller coaster ride. Oil and gas prices plummeted but have inched back up in recent years. U.S. dependency on foreign oil supply remains above 50 percent, leading some observers to say the U.S. can be held hostage again to exorbitant oil prices that would fuel inflation. The turmoil created by Iraq's invasion of Kuwait is vivid evidence of these prophecies.

Although the U.S.'s East and West Coasts have suffered the least from these events, real estate has been depressed generally. Real estate values in places like Houston were devastated by the combination of falling oil prices and the failures of banks and savings and loans, but values have continued to rise at dizzying rates in places like San Diego.

And the savings and loans mess continues to grow. It is estimated that the bailout will cost each U.S. citizen about $2,000 or more over the next 30 to 40 years. Such reports are political dynamite, so politicians are running for cover as the public mood on this issue grows angrier.

Although other events could be cited, these prominent ones cloud the future of financial institutions. And these institutions are TEI's bread-and-butter clients. It is generally believed that the leadership of most financial institutions is at a loss as to how to position and promote themselves. This confusion can mean they may be less inclined to buy new equipment, embrace new technologies and so on, therefore jeopardizing TEI's future.

Major TEI Players

The largest stockholder in TEI is Oscar T. House. He is also chairman of the board of directors. He founded what became TEI in 1970 when he began his research and development of the first ATM. He has BS and MS degrees in mechanical engineering from the Massachusetts Institute of Technology. He worked as a professional engineer for 10 years after earning his MS degree.

House got interested in the banking industry quite by accident. He was part of a design team assigned to evaluate the plans for a new major bank building in Philadelphia. In the course of his work on that team, he became personal friends with the operations manager of the new bank. As they talked casually over a drink about the problems related to serving bank customers well with such limited lobby hours, the idea of a remote teller was spawned.

House quit his job two months later, borrowed all the money he could and went to work in the basement of his Chicago home. He has a father's pride in his offspring, the ATM, but he's even prouder of TEI, especially of how it is perceived as a reliable, trustworthy company by the financial community it serves. He's been spending a lot more time than usual at corporate headquarters in Orlando, Florida. Close associates say he's really worried about TEI's future.

The president and chief executive officer is Carla L. Chase. She's an electronics genius whose chip designs are widely respected. She's been in these posts four years, having come to TEI from a Silicon Valley firm, where she was vice president of research and development. She's said to be innovative and is expected to produce new products for TEI, although to date none has her stamp.

Her BS, MS and PhD degrees are all in electrical engineering from the California Institute of Technology. Associates say she is bright, but a little snappy with people and is sometimes withdrawn. Even key managers have difficulty getting in to see her now and then.

Brewster P. Phleuger is vice president for marketing and communications. Phleuger has a BS in botany from Iowa State University. He earned his MBA at Northwestern University. Because of his interest in research and his skill in statistics, he went to work with the Opinion Research Corporation as a project analyst. He rose through the ranks to become its vice president of public affairs. He joined TEI seven years ago. He is House's personal friend and most upper-level employees at TEI say Phleuger is listened to more carefully than anyone else in the organization.

Personal Notes about TEI -

Personal Notes about Scenarios -

Quick-Study 1

Extract, Chapter 1, "Public Relations and the Writer," *Public Relations Writing: Form & Style* 3e, Belmont, California: Wadsworth, 1991

Y ou must first reconcile the two senses in which the term *public relations* is used. The *general sense* simply describes the art of getting along with people. The *professional sense* describes the art of *brokering goodwill* between an organization and its publics. Good writing usually plays a central role in the brokering process.

That is because good public relations writers play many roles. They must be able *to identify and identify with priority or target audiences*, adapt *appropriate writing styles*, write messages to *fit the format* of the media used to deliver them and shape their messages, without distortion, so the messages are *acceptable* to target audiences.

Be careful as a beginning writer to avoid the synonymous use of the terms *advertising, publicity* and *public relations*. They are not the same things. The following points may help you sort out some main differences among these terms:

1. *Advertising is media time or space bought to carry and distribute the buyer's message.* In effect, buyers lease this time or space so they can control what, when, how and how often messages go to target audiences. It is communication in one direction.

2. *Publicity is information given without charge or payment to the media.* Its use, if any, is at the discretion of editors of the media, not yours. It is also one-way communication.

3. *Public relations communication is two-way communication* that may, and often does, use advertising and publicity, but significantly public relations seeks the mutual benefits of interacting and exchanging information with mass and specialized media and audiences. The media and public relations share a common goal: *to engage their respective audiences in sustained relationships.* Good writers are key players in these situations.

Audiences are people tied together by common bonds. Understanding how and why these bonds are formed is a fundamental challenge to all writers. Research can uncover demographic and psychographic information that can help writers to understand attitudes, beliefs, values and behaviors. Without this understanding, they guess. They may guess wrong.

Good writers also know they must shape their messages one way for a particular public and in a different way for another public. Some audiences are more important than others to their organizations. These are *priority* audiences and writers focus their messages on those groups. That process is called *targeting the message to the audience.*

Good public relations writers also must intimately know the organizations they work for, the audiences most important to their organizations and the channels of communication to which these audiences pay the most attention. All of this is necessary to write *effectively and efficiently in all appropriate media pertinent to audiences.* The first commandment of public relations writing is: *Know your audience.*

EXERCISES

All Scenarios 1 : 1

Review the scenario assigned to you or, if you are working independently, selected by you. Make a list of all the possible publics related to the scenario. Be as detailed as possible. Remember the rule from the preceding Quick-Study: *Know your audience.* It is impossible to make too detailed a list. Then group the publics by type, such as government, which should be further divided into local, state and national. Turn in the assignment on the due date.

Independent 1 : 1

Do what's described above but focus the list on the college you attend or attended. If you've been away from campus some time, select a profit or non-profit organization in your community and complete the exercise.

All Scenarios and Independent 1 : 2

Study your list from Assignment 1:1. Which of these publics is most important to the organization? Least important? The information in Table 1-1 in *PRW3e* will help you derive answers systematically. Rank-order the list so the most important public is listed first, the second most important is listed second and so on. Write a brief but detailed report (three or four paragraphs) that explains why you listed these publics in that order. Turn in the assignment on the due date.

All Scenarios and Independent 1 : 3

Refer to the public you listed as the most important in Assignment 1:2. Think about the people who make up that public. What holds them together as a group? What are they like as individuals? What do they do for a living? How do they spend their free time? What issues are important to them? Feel free to add your own questions.

Write a summary memo of your conclusions about this public to Ms. Kari M. Backe, account services supervisor at ProCom. This is an important memo because the account team will review it later when they write for a client. The date on the memo should be the same as the due date for this assignment.

Notes -

Quick-Study 2

Extract, Chapter 2, "Ethical and Legal Responsibilities of the Writer," *Public Relations Writing: Form & Style* 3e, Belmont, California: Wadsworth, 1991

Y ou must be sensitive to the feelings and needs of others, and treat them as you want to be treated by them. This sensitivity exerts its greatest influence in the way you and the organization for which you work perceive something as *right* or *wrong*. If these perceptions don't align generally with those of your relevant audiences, *credibility* may be jeopardized. If you or your organization loses credibility, neither you nor your organization will be very successful.

The right or wrong of a situation may have little or nothing to do with facts or truth or what may be defined in laws, regulations or rules. That's because people's *perceptions are their realities*. Even if the *explicit messages* you write are factual and truthful, they may be contradicted by the *implicit messages* audiences perceive in your organization's behavior.

Remember that how relevant audiences perceive your organization is more likely to be based on the *consequences* of what your organization *does* than on what you *say* about it. If your organization operates outside the limits of your audience's acceptable standards, what you say or do may make little difference to them. You have a special professional responsibility in such cases to reconcile these differences to the mutual benefit of your organization and its publics. That task often isn't easy.

Your personal and professional sense of ethical and socially responsible behavior plays a key role in how you perform as a writer. If you are in tune with the standards of your organization, the public relations industry and your audience, you'll find your job easier. If you are out of step, your job will be more difficult.

Your real worth to your organization is knowing the limits of what its relevant audiences view as acceptable behavior and staying well within them. You must make regular and sustained efforts to keep in touch with relevant audiences. Only then can you expect to construct messages both valuable and acceptable to them.

You will work in a litigation-happy environment. You must protect yourself and your organization by bulletproofing your writing as much as possible. Legal actions can be brought at any time for any reason. So you may not always avoid them, but you can keep them from being successful. Pay particular attention to the laws of libel, defamation of character and slander, contracts, contempt, privacy and copyright. If you have doubts about how to say something or even if something should be said, consult an attorney specializing in communication law.

Also keep up with rulings from the Postal Service, the Federal Trade Commission, the Securities and Exchange Commission or similar governmental bodies that deal with the industry of which your organization is a part.

One important point to remember about laws and regulations is that they are always in *flux*. What is legally and ethically permissible today may not be so tomorrow. Another is that laws are generally *negative*.

EXERCISES

All Scenarios and Independent 2 : 1

The office of public information at State University yesterday, in response to persistent rumors during the last few days, confirmed that Melody S. Hanzout, daughter of U.S. Senator Herchel H. Hanzout, has been awarded a full scholarship (tuition, fees, books, supplies, room and board) to finish her fifth year of study at the university. She has maintained a 3.6 grade point average (on a 4.0 scale) during her first four years of study.

The managing editor of the *Clarion* assigned a reporter to interview Ms. Hanzout because the Hanzout family is widely known around Serene. Early in the interview Ms. Hanzout expressed some dismay at having gotten a scholarship because she had never applied for one. This prompted the reporter to wonder why the scholarship had been awarded. Contacts were made with several people.

The president of the university, Dr. T. A. Lott, said that Ms. Hanzout was singled out as a deserving student and the university simply wanted to acknowledge her scholarship. When asked if the scholarship award was made to curry favor from her father, the U.S. Senator, Lott said, "Certainly not. We don't try to buy influence."

The director of student financial aid, Edgar M. Burns, said Ms. Hanzout deserved the scholarship not only for her scholarly record but also for her leadership as president last year of her sorority, Alpha Alpha Alpha. He pointed out she had also been active in a number of Greek activities throughout her tenure at the university.

When asked if it was common to award scholarships to students who had not applied, Burns said, "It has happened before, but not often. We try to make sure scholarship money goes to deserving applicants only." When asked who made the decision to award the scholarship, Burns said the decision was made "higher up" and the word came in a telephone conversation, but he couldn't remember from whom. Asked to name other students who had been given scholarships, he declined to say, indicating that privacy laws prevented such disclosures.

Several members of the scholarship application review committee denied any knowledge of the scholarship awarded to Ms. Hanzout. The chair, Professor Damon R. Philley, said she is appalled by the cavalier way the scholarship was awarded. She pledged that her committee would immediately look into the matter.

Senator Hanzout was away from his Washington office on a fact-finding tour to the Middle East, but Hanzout's press aide, Montgomery (Monty) F. Peace, responded to phone questions from the *Clarion* reporter that Senator Hanzout is proud of his daughter and her accomplishments and is especially pleased about her scholarship.

Senator Hanzout was also reported to have said the university is a fine one and he's very glad his daughter is a student there. Peace also confirmed that Hanzout expects to be named chair of the U. S. Senate's education subcommittee next year. The current chairman has announced he will not seek office after his current term ends this year.

The story in yesterday's *Clarion* caused an uproar on campus. The chair of the university's faculty senate called an emergency meeting of the executive committee and at noon issued a strongly worded statement that condemned the university's action. The statement also carried a muted inference that Lott should resign from the presidency.

The executive committee of student government also met briefly and issued a similar statement. But the student government statement openly called for resignations from both Lott and Burns. Lott issued a prepared statement today at 1 P.M., the text of which reads:

The scholarship awarded to Ms. Melody S. Hanzout
was given in recognition of her outstanding scho-
lastic record and her achievements as a leading
citizen of the university community. It is the
standing policy of the university to recognize students in many ways for their achievements. I am
not sure personally who made the decision to award
the scholarship but it was a good decision. Because there seems to be some concern about it, my
office today has launched an investigation into the
process by which all scholarship decisions are
made.

Lott today did not take or return phone calls from the media. Even when Burns took media calls, he responded to all questions with "No comment." Unconfirmed reports say several media representatives appear to be camped just outside the president's office.

Other than staff members, only two people, I. M. Professor and Ms. Kari M. Backe of ProCom, have been allowed into Lott's suite. Rumor has it that Lott called them in as consultants to assist him with the problem. A student protest march around the administration building at 4 p.m. today has been called by the student government president.

The phone rings at your desk at ProCom. It is Ms. Backe calling from Lott's office. She directs you to get together with the other writers at ProCom and research the situation at the University. "We're in Lott's office now. As you know, it has really hit the fan. We may be here well into the evening while we try to sort out strategic approaches to a solution to the problem. What Professor and I want you to do is to research the legal and ethical dimensions of the problem. Hit the law books and other sources and give us a summary of your findings. Your research may uncover other questions, but look at these for starters:

1. What legal requirements must be observed?

2. Is it better to try to cover up an unseemly situation than to face it squarely? What is the rationale for either decision?

3. What are the university's obligations to Ms. Hanzout and to its relevant publics, such as students, faculty and staff?

4. What ethical questions must be resolved?

5. Do ethical and legal issues conflict in this instance? If so, how can they be resolved?"

Then Backe directs you to write a two-page summary of relevant findings and have it ready for review at 7 A.M. tomorrow. "We'll finish the strategy discussion with Lott this afternoon or evening," she said, "but we won't implement anything until we've thoroughly studied your report. Your purpose is to keep us and Lott from making a serious mistake. Ciao."

Notes -

Quick-Study 3

Extract, Chapter 3, "Persuasion," *Public Relations Writing: Form & Style* 3e, Belmont, California: Wadsworth, 1991

Persuading someone to adopt your point of view is difficult and complex. That's because behavior has rational and emotional dimensions. Being rational means people can think for themselves. They may choose, for whatever reasons, to think things or in ways that makes your job harder. Persuasion is your only recourse because you can't make audiences comply.

You must figure out how to persuade your audience that your way or view about an issue is sounder, clearer, more reasonable perhaps than theirs. That sounds simple, but it isn't. There are no surefire ways to persuade people (unless you're a used car salesperson), but a few guidelines may help.

Learn everything you can about human behavior. Remember, only a few basic persuasive strategies exist, although many variations of each one are possible. Choose the strategic approach best suited to your purpose. Always make this choice from the point of view of your audience.

If your purpose is merely to gain simple audience awareness and association, a *stimulus-response* approach may work. If you're dealing with a sophisticated audience likely to be skeptical of what you're saying, consider a *cognitive* strategy. If an appeal to an audience's self-interest will meet your purpose, then a *motivational* approach may work, but only if you show your audience an attainable, desirable reward.

If individuals in your target audience identify strongly with group norms, a strategy based on *social* relationships may be best. A *personality* strategy may work if your target audience is made up of people who see themselves as real individualists. But this last strategy is hard to execute because it is difficult to make a message personal when it goes to millions. Consult Chapter 3 in *PRW3e* for detailed explanations of these strategies.

Even if you use the right strategy, you may fail if you don't pay attention to the steps in the persuasion process. If you skip a step, you're less effective. You must reach people at the *right time and place,* with the *right message* and in the *right form* if you expect audiences to pay *attention.* They won't *understand* what you want them to know if you don't get their attention. And they may not *accept* what you say, even if they understand it completely. You also must *reinforce* their acceptance long enough for them to take the *action* you want.

How your organization presents an issue or program must match closely what you say about it. You lose *credibility* when actions and words don't coincide. You won't be believed. In fact, you may be mistrusted. Remember also that some media have more credibility than others.

Determine when and under what conditions you should give only your side of an issue. Other important decisions in the persuasion process include which side should be given first, whether the good or bad news should be shared first and whether an explicit conclusion is preferred over letting an audience draw its own.

Pay particular attention to how or even if you should appeal to your audience's fears, especially in the context of social issues and political campaigns. And learn as much as you can about when it is best to use rational or emotional appeals or a combination of both.

The spoken word is generally more persuasive than the written word. But the written word seems to produce more understanding than the spoken. Opinion leaders are generally more media-dependent than most audience members. Many persuasive efforts seen in the media are filtered through opinion leaders, so how the message influences the broader audience is often an indirect process. If you want to sensitize the public to an issue, you must get it on the public agenda through the media.

Time may be your best ally when your organization suffers a loss in public confidence. People tend to forget. This tendency also means that you must keep reminding people about your organization. If you do, it is easier to deal successfully with audiences when problems arise unexpectedly.

What you write begins with an implicit persuasive purpose. Disguising your intent may hamper the way you write and muddle your messages. What you gain in acceptance by disguising your purpose may be more than offset by losses in levels of audience attention and understanding.

EXERCISES

All Scenarios and Independent 3 : 1

Review the situation described in Assignment 2:1. Dr. T. A. Lott, president of State University in Serene, had called in Professor and Backe from ProCom for advice on how to handle the problem of the scholarship awarded to Melody Hanzout.

Ms. Backe had asked you to provide a brief the next morning for her and the Professor to review before they gave the go-ahead to Lott on the strategy worked out the night before. Professor and Backe reviewed your brief and found nothing in it to suggest the chosen strategy would be a mistake. When Professor called Lott to give him the green light, President Lott became hostile. Some of his comments follow:

"You really expect me to say and do those things? Why, the students, faculty and alumni will crucify me and the university. I am the leader of this university. It has too many friends in positions of influence to allow harm to come to it. You people just don't know much about how the academic mind works."

"This is really just a tempest in a teapot. It will blow over soon. I should have followed my own judgment in the first place. I've turned the matter over to Mann (Y. S. Mann, director of information at the University) who knows how to do what I tell him."

"You can send me your invoice for the services you didn't render to me and I'll see about getting it paid—sometime." With that, President Lott hung up the phone. Professor leaned back and laughed loudly in disbelief.

Mann called a press conference at 11 A.M. at which time he issued a news release quoted on page 56.

Dr. T. A. Lott, president of State University, announced this morning that no consideration will be given to revoking the scholarship awarded to Melody S. Hanzout of Serene. The scholarship became the focus of protests yesterday by faculty and students when a *Clarion* reporter revealed Ms. Hanzout had not applied for a scholarship.

"This whole affair has been blown out of proportion by muckraking media and misguided people who really don't understand the nature of the university's scholarship program," Lott said.

President Lott has also called for a full investigation into the way applicants are evaluated and how scholarships are awarded.

"If mistakes in our scholarship program have been made, we must know about them so we can correct them," he said.

"But under no circumstances will Melody's scholarship be rescinded," he continued, "because she's already suffered enough abuse at the hands of the media and insensitive supporters of the university."

A full investigation of the scholarship program will take two to three months to complete, says Y. S. Mann, director of information. "President Lott is anxious to see the final report so steps can be taken to prevent problems similar to this one," Mann said.

Mann then fielded questions from reporters for about five minutes. Some of his responses follow.

"No, Melody emphatically was not given the scholarship because of the potential influence her father can
bring to bear on behalf of the University. That is
patently absurd, and an insult to Senator Hanzout and
President Lott."

"Yes, Dr. Lott is very concerned about the whole
affair and determined to resolve it quickly and equi-
tably."

"No, Dr. Lott thinks it's funny that some people
are calling for his scalp. And he certainly does not
intend to give it to them willingly."

"Ms. Hanzout is an outstanding student whose record
fully justifies the scholarship awarded to her. That
she did not apply for it in no way means she does not
deserve it. She represents the very kind of student
the university seeks to recruit."

"Dr. Lott will make no further statements about
this matter until the final report on the scholarship
program evaluation is complete. Thank you for coming.
If I can be of further help, call me."

Professor assigns you to review and analyze carefully the content of the university's news release and Mann's comments to reporters. "Even if ProCom is no longer related to this client," Professor explains, "you'll learn a lot about persuasion by looking at what is going on out there now. So write me a brief report (about two double-spaced pages) and have it on my desk tomorrow in time for our regular meeting." Professor goes on to suggest that, among others, the report should consider the following questions:

1. Which persuasive strategy(ies) is (are) most apparent in the news release and statements at the press conference? Explain why it (they) will or will not work.

2. Which step(s) in the persuasive process may be jeopardized most by the strategy(ies) used?

3. What other persuasive communication flaw(s) can you spot in the way Lott and Mann are handling this problem?

4. Is another strategic approach better? If so, which one and why do you recommend it?

Notes -

Quick-Study 4

Extract, Chapter 4, "Research for the Public Relations Writer," *Public Relations Writing: Form & Style* 3e, Belmont, California: Wadsworth, 1991

Public relations writers depend on information generated from research. The less they know about something, the more they need research. The more they research something, the more likely they are to recognize what they don't know. Knowing what they don't know is the first step toward enlightenment. Filling those information gaps with credible data helps them avoid mistakes.

Good writers know, at least instinctively, that they'll make more mistakes when they write about something that stretches the limits of their knowledge about a topic. Aside from topic-specific knowledge, the research most writers do focuses on six broad areas: policy, background material, audience, message, media and program evaluation.

Research information is useless if it can't be retrieved quickly. That's why most writers form personal habits of routinely filing away information for later use. They also know where and how to get the needed information not already in their offices. They may spend a good bit of time in libraries poring over journals and reference books or gleaning information from flickering images on microfilm or microfiche readers. They also may dial electronic data bases and call up what they need. Clearly, the source or form of the information is not as important as knowing where and how to get it.

The information needed in most public relations writing situations already exists. Searching existing information is called *secondary research*. It is secondary not because it is unimportant but because it was developed elsewhere for other purposes, and your potential use of it is secondary to its original intent.

Even when writers know that information is available, they sometimes don't recognize it when they see it. It is like wondering why manhole covers are round. Everyone who took geometry in high school knows why, but most people don't make the connection, at least immediately.

A circular manhole cover is the only geometric shape that won't fall into the hole if it is dislodged by traffic. What's the point? Writers must be able to synthesize information. They must see relationships between seemingly unrelated concepts or data.

When information is not already available, you must do *primary research*. Its most common forms are interviews and surveys. However, you must still turn to secondary information to prepare carefully for the questions you do ask. Otherwise, your interview or survey won't elicit the information you need from your primary research.

Secondary or primary data are often in statistical form and much data have been developed from samples. If the sample was not randomly chosen and is not truly representative, then the data generated should not be generalized about your entire audience.

Be skeptical if research protocols (noted in Example 4-4, p. 70, *PRW3e*) are missing or are so vaguely worded you can't see exactly how the information was developed. It may be good information, but it also may be bad. Good writers cross-check information. Just because a source says something is true does not make it so. It is only when several sources generally say the same thing that you can be reasonably sure of the accuracy, meaning and reliability of the information.

One of the most common writing projects in PR is the *fact sheet*, a compendium of the findings from a range of continuing research efforts. Its value can be enormous if it is current, accurate and complete.

EXERCISES

FNB 4 : 1

Review scholarly journals as well as popular journals and newspapers for articles on banking and finance written in the last five years. Search for pieces that provide insights into such questions as:

1. Why did so many banks fail?

2. Why did so many savings and loans fail?

3. What changes in rules and regulations have been made in the banking and savings and loans industries as a result of these failures?

4. What are the best guesses regarding when the banking and savings and loan industries will return to normal?

5. Which of these changes may affect the First National Bank of Serene?

Write a report of no more than four pages, typed or word-processed and double-spaced, summarizing your findings. Turn it in on the due date.

NATS 4 : 1

Review scholarly and trade journals, as well as popular journals, of the last three years that deal with the medical profession in general and emergency medicine specifically. Search for articles and reports that describe the kinds of problems faced by institutions and people specializing in giving emergency care. Look for information that gives insights into issues such as:

1. Reasons why emergency care costs are skyrocketing.

2. Patterns of behavior of emergency medicine caregivers.

3. Effects of malpractice suits, not just on costs, but also on policies, of institutions and the related behavior of emergency medicine caregivers.

4. Problems related to getting more physicians to specialize in emergency medicine.

Write a report of no more than four pages, typed or word-processed and double-spaced, summarizing your findings. Turn it in on the due date.

NCCC 4 : 1

Research the scholarly and trade literature of the last three years that deals with day-care trends and developments. Look especially for information that gives insights into such issues as:

1. The growing need for day-care programs and facilities.

2. Which factors are most important in predicting trends in the day-care industry.

3. Why entrepreneurs have entered the day-care business.

4. How child development programs can be integrated into day-care services.

5. What kinds of staff credentials must be sought if developmental programs are part of day-care operations.

Write a report of no more than four pages, typed or word-processed and double-spaced, summarizing your findings. Turn it in on the due date.

TEI 4 : 1

Research the industries that sell supplies and equipment to financial institutions. Scan scholarly and trade journals of the last three years to get insights into such issues as:

1. Technological innovations that make it possible for banks and savings and loans to provide a broader range of services to clients through remote devices such as ATMs, drive-throughs, home-sited computer-based transactions and the like.

2. Why a firm like TEI must be concerned with the overall economic health of the industries it serves.

3. How hardware, such as the ATM 2001, can open up new avenues for marketing banking services.

4. The role software research and development can play in TEI's marketing strategies.

Write a report of no more than four pages, typed or word-processed and double-spaced, summarizing your findings. Turn it in on the due date.

Independent 4 : 1

Read scholarly and trade journals of the last three years that deal with scholarship and financial aids programs in higher education. Also get as much information as you can from the scholarships and financial aids office at your own university. Treat this information as if it is from the scholarships and financial aids office at Serene's State University. Also review the scholarship situation at State University as described in Assignments 2 : 1 and 3 : 1. Write a report on the status of the scholarship and financial aids programs at State University, paying special attention to issues such as:

1. University-wide scholarship policies.

2. Criteria for certain scholarships imposed by donors.

3. How and to what extent equity is maintained throughout the scholarship program.

4. Whether the scholarship and financial aids program at State University is adequate to support students who must have help to get through their degree programs.

5. The level of confidence faculty, staff, students and donors have in the way the scholarship and financial program is administered.

Write a report of no more than four pages, typed or word-processed and double-spaced, summarizing your findings. Turn it in on the due date.

All Scenarios and Independent 4 : 2

Consider the research report prepared in Assignment 4 : 1. Write a two-page, typed or word-processed, double-spaced report that describes what you believe may be important information that you could not find. Suggest where this information might be found and how you propose to get it. Turn it in on the due date.

Notes -

Quick-Study 5

Extract, Chapter 5, "Writing for Clarity and Interest," *Public Relations Writing: Form & Style* 3e, Belmont, California: Wadsworth, 1991

The most common mistake beginning public relations writers make is that they try to tell everything they know. Learn the art of leaving your audience with only one provocative thought. Not two, three or more. Just one. Before you can master that art, you must first learn to observe three important rules:

1. Know your message.

2. Know your audience.

3. Know which medium the audience is most likely to tune in to.

If you can't write a simple declarative sentence that clearly spells out your message, then think about it some more before you begin to write. Once you know exactly what the message is, you must look at it from the audience's point of view. Shape the message in ways that conform to your audience's expectations and needs. And write it for the medium that will carry it to the audience.

These rules suggest how to think about writing, not how to write. Other rules apply to the art of writing. For example, you must write two or three grade levels below the limits of your audience's understanding. This is not to suggest that you write down to the audience, but merely that you write your message so it is more likely to be read, seen or listened to.

Study the information in Example 5:1, which presents the results of a Flesch readability analysis of this Quick-Study. Average sentence length is just under 14 words. The reading-ease score means about 63 percent of all adults can read this section without difficulty. Readability is equal to ninth-grade level reading skills. Writing that impresses audiences is writing they can understand with relative ease. Remember you can't command an audience's attention. Your only choice is to write so audiences will volunteer their attention.

Study the readability formulas in Appendix A of *PRW3e*. Although each has its unique approach, the formulas share some features. Each focuses on average sentence and word lengths. Audiences generally will read more if you write sentences of between 14 and 17 words. And the use of short, familiar words get more attention and understanding than the use of long, unfamiliar ones.

Good writing also sounds natural, conversational. Although written for the eye, when it is read aloud good writing sounds good. You should also vary sentence structure, and remember active voice is more provocative than passive. Writing that has a natural rhythm is more pleasant and tempting to read than stilted prose, and is more

---

Example 5:1—Readability Analysis

This Flesch readability analysis was done automatically by the software program Sensible Grammar™.

Readability Analysis: XB Quick-Study 5

TUE OCT 29, 1991 12:34:28 P.M.

Total Sentences:	44	Total Words:	552
Average Sentence Length:		12.54	
Average Syllables Per Word:		1.47	

Reading Ease: Standard   Flesch

Readable For % Adults: 63%

0%   50%   100%

Readable Grade Level: 9th

4   5   6   7   8   9   10   11   12   College   Grad

Human Interest: Interesting   25%

0%   50%   100%

likely to move audiences, especially if the writing has strong human interest value. And good writing avoids trite expressions.

One of the dramatic changes in modern writing style is its gender-free quality. Professional writers and media understand that sex bias in writing turns off many readers, viewers and listeners. This applies equally to ethnic, age or other biases. *All* audience members expect to be treated fairly, and they should be. Be cautious about letting bias slip by. Even if the slip is inadvertent, it is no less hurtful in an audience's collective mind. Watch it.

Removing biases also improves writing and makes it easier to read. That is a win-win situation. And it isn't difficult to do. Just follow a few common-sense rules, as seen in Example 5:2, p. 100, in *PRW3e*.

EXERCISES

All Scenarios and Independent 5 : 1

Improving your descriptive powers is essential if you want to become a good writer. Being able to describe something clearly, effectively depends on being a keen observer. Think of the times you've laughed or cried, felt relieved or apprehensive, excited or depressed. What happened to cause those feelings? Can you describe them to others so they become "real"? Good writers can. To stretch your descriptive powers, write a paragraph of no more than 35 words for each of *any five* of the ideas, concepts or events in the list below. Your purpose is to make readers feel, taste, smell or see what you describe.

1. The touch of a just-bathed human body.

2. The scent of a rosebud (any color) in the early morning.

3. The taste of double chocolate mocha (or your favorite flavor) ice cream.

4. The smell of a new car's interior.

5. The love you feel for a significant other (not the physical act of making love).

6. The sight or smell of a wet, long-haired dog.

7. A maple leaf falling to the ground on an autumn morning.

8. The comfort of a favorite pair of jeans.

9. The tingle in your nose as you begin drinking a carbonated soda.

Try to use two sentences in each description. Do not use the word *experience* in any guise. But have some fun with this exercise because there is no right way to do it. Remember you're trying to get others to experience something through your writing. Expect to make several false starts on every description. Once you complete a draft, set it aside. Come back to it a day later and do whatever editing and rewriting is needed.

FNB 5 : 2

Visit a bank lobby for about 30 minutes. Take note of its physical layout, its decor, the kinds of transactions you observe taking place, and so on. Be sure to tell someone in the lobby what you're doing. For example, contact the people at the customer information or new accounts desks. Then write a one-page, single-spaced, typed or word-processed description of what you saw. Your description should be complete and clear enough that anyone could recognize the lobby from what you have written, even if they had never seen it before. Turn in the assignment on the due date.

NATS 5 : 2

Set up a 30-minute interview with a person whose career is in one of the following fields: health care, fire fighting or prevention, police or criminal justice or emergency services (any type). Your goal is to get from the interviewee recollections of the worst or best situation she or he encountered in that field. Ask probing questions, and listen carefully to responses, especially to the adjectives used to describe the situation. Take extensive notes. When you finish, write a one-page, single-spaced, typed or word-processed description of what the interviewee recalled. Help the reader "see" or "feel" what the interviewee shared with you. Turn in the description on the due date.

TEI 5 : 2

Write a one-page, single-spaced, typed or word-processed description of what it is like to withdraw $50 from a capricious ATM. Assume it either gives you five $1 bills instead of five $10 bills or spits out fifty $10.00 bills. Also cyborg logic properly debits your account with a $50 withdrawal. You can have some fun with this, but keep the description of your reactions within the realm of reality. If you choose the second instance, don't overlook the issue of personal ethics in your description.

NCCC 5 : 2

Preschool children often do funny things. Visit a church nursery, day-care center or a kindergarten and watch the children carefully. Make sure you call the person in charge ahead of time and get permission to be at the location for about an hour. Introduce yourself to the adults when you get to the site, and explain what you're doing. Then blend into the background. Take notes about what the children are doing. Be especially attentive to how they interact with one another. Look for signs of aggressive or passive behavior. Observe how these behaviors relate to their activities. Write a one-page, single-spaced, typed or word-processed description of what you saw. What you want to convey is what the world is like from a child's point of view. Turn in the report on the due date.

Independent 5 : 2

Attend a session of the student government body on your campus. If you're not now on a campus, attend a school board, city council or similar meeting. Note what people say, but especially observe their body language, voice inflection and pitch as they speak, and so on. Note aggressive or passive behavior. Evaluate to what extent nonverbal behavior matches or contradicts what is said. Write a description of observed behavior. It should be one page, single-spaced and typed or word-processed. Remember your purpose is to get your reader to "feel" that she or he was at the meeting. Turn in the assignment on the due date.

Notes -

Quick-Study 6

Extract, Chapter 6, "Simplifying the Complex," *Public Relations Writing: Form & Style* 3e, Belmont, California: Wadsworth, 1991

O ne of the great challenges in public relations is to write simply about complex topics. And that approach is most often exactly what is expected of you. Simplifying the complex isn't as difficult as it may sound. Observe a few rules.

First and foremost, *know your subject*. That means you must research the topic thoroughly. It does not mean that you must be a scientist to explain quantum physics, for example, to lay audiences. Part of your research effort must be devoted to understanding the jargon common to the topic. Only if you understand the jargon can you ask the right questions of experts in the field. If you don't ask good questions, you may not understand the answers you get. If you don't get "it," how will you explain it to audiences who don't have specialized knowledge? What you don't know may make you dangerous to yourself and to your audience.

Another rule is to *use plain English*. Although you must understand the jargon of the field about which you're writing, avoid using that jargon in what you write for people outside the field. Most people understand standard English. And that's what they expect and yearn for when they're reading outside their own fields.

To use plain English is to *avoid doublespeak*. Doublespeak is generally writing to impress, not to communicate. It is sometimes used deliberately to deceive. One of its devices is the *euphemism*. This tactic substitutes a more "pleasant" word or phrase for a more resolute one. For example, "She passed away" rather than "She died." Successful politicians hone the use of euphemisms to high art.

Also, don't use *fancy words* instead of simple ones because the result inflates or obscures meaning. *Gobbledygook* is the linguistic legacy of modern bureaucracy. It is bureaucratese writ large and often. It favors phrases like "parameters to work within" when "specific limits" is plainer, simpler and easier to understand.

Publishers tell textbook writers to define, then describe, when they introduce new concepts. But that's about the only time you should write that way, which introduces the next rule on simplifying the complex: *describe, don't define.* Using precise, technically correct definitions in your writing shows you know what you're talking about. But not only must you be correct, you must also communicate with your audience. You do that by describing concepts in terms audiences understand. Develop your descriptive powers if you expect to succeed in simplifying complex ideas.

Not only must you describe, you must also feed new information in small bites to your audience. That means observing another rule: *take one step at a time.* Don't overload your writing with too much new information too quickly. That turns off readers.

You also turn off readers if you don't observe yet another rule for simplifying the complex: *make the central point clear.* Tell readers at the beginning what your point is. This not only gives them a context in which to evaluate what you say later, it gives them a sense of anticipation about what follows.

A final rule is to *explain the unfamiliar with the familiar.* Analogies that tap your audience's common experiences are your best ally when simplifying the complex. This point is sharply illustrated in Example 6-3, p. 117, *PRW3e.* Study it carefully to see how analogy can reduce a complex idea to a level that anyone can understand.

Before you tackle the next assignment, read and study carefully the content of Example 6:1 of this text. Wank's plaintive message is more and more common in the public relations field.

Example 6:1—Appeal for Better Writers

Martin Wank is president of Wank Associates in Greenvale, New York. His comments reflect a plea expressed more and more often. Take with utter seriousness the necessity of learning to write well.

Wanted: Writers who can at least write

By Martin Wank

Writing is a big part of the public relations profession. But agencies and companies seeking writers face an almost insurmountable challenge these days. What goes by the name of writer is usually a dreaming wanderer lost in a maze of meaningless words. There are many aspirants but few accomplished candidates.

One job candidate told me that the baby-boom generation, of which she was a part, never learned anything about writing in college. When I countered that my agency's work required thinking even more than writing, she laughed and said her generation knew less about thinking than about writing (herself excepted).

Two employees we hired and fired last year were graduates of the master's degree program in technology writing given by a well-known technical university in New York City. One had an undergraduate degree in mathematics. These candidates are just for us, I had thought, since we specialize in high technology, so we hired them. But we found that they could not write anything beyond a form of vernacular that imitated speech among their peers. Loose phrases used in everyday life appeared routinely in their copy—but it was not copy; that word should be reserved for professional writing. In addition, they knew absolutely nothing about the business world and could not seem to get straight what factories do within their walls. They knew that products were manufactured there; how was a mystery, even though that knowledge was essential to our work.

One of the employees, a man about 30 years old, was on the way to becoming a carbon copy of Melville's "Bartleby the Scrivener" when he was fired. He took pleasure in hanging around the office, but did not work beyond constantly perusing papers. (He often wrote the redundant formulation: "perusing through . . . ") When I told him the jig was up, he said nothing. When I stood up to usher him out, he remained seated. When I opened the door as an invitation to leave, he remained as he was.

Later, I interviewed a writing teacher from the undergraduate faculty of the same university. I told him about these two past employees and let them off easy by saying that they had studied on the graduate level. Not much difference, the teacher said. The undergraduates are terrible writers and are no better when they leave than when they arrive. He was not surprised that a master's degree in writing from his institution did not improve their skills.

What ails the supposed writers in our business, or those who are trying to get into our business? They know nothing about the structure of a piece of writing and have no idea that a piece of writing contains a structure. (Some of them

(Continued on Page 72.)

Example 6:1 (Continued)

have been taught a bit about forms—the interview, the inverted pyramid—but nothing about internal structure.)

They believe that writing is simply a progression from whatever beginning they choose to whenever they run out of gas. Running out of gas constitutes the end of the piece. After 10 years of searching, I have seen virtually no one who deigns to pen a conclusion—what one job candidate brightly termed "a kicker."

They do not know that a piece of writing has to have a forceful point, however much the force may be hidden from view. They resist absolutely writing what is needed; they believe that they are hired to write what they like, which should be sufficient to fill the bill. Only they do not know what the "bill" is; that is, the purpose of the piece they are trying to write—even though you will tell them over and over and prepare them and instruct them in every conceivable way, showing them countless examples of what is expected. When you instruct them, I have found, they mentally look out the window. Their minds are turned off. They are at the beach if it is summer, skiing if it is winter. They are also mildly amused at the entire instruction process, as though they were observers, not participants.

There has been a flurry of books about failing education systems in the U.S., and America's weakened economic position in the world, and how these two are related. Believe it. If what I have seen in trying to recruit writers (for what is after all a small public relations agency) reflects what is happening out there, we are just at the beginning of the bad news. Somebody up there does not want to tell us the whole truth all at once.

Source: *Advertising Age*, February 18, 1991, p. 25. Used with permission of Martin Wank.

EXERCISES

FNB 6 : 1

Below is a description of the business of banking at First National Bank, Serene. It is written at about the 16th grade level. A college senior should read and understand it with little effort. Study the underlined jargon words and concepts. Go to the library and see what you can find out about them. When you feel you understand them, rewrite the description as a one-page, typed or word-processed, double-spaced report about the business of banking at First National Bank, Serene. Your report will be duplicated and distributed Wednesday to an 11th grade social studies class at Serene High School. Remember your audience, and write to its level. Thus, lower the reading skill level to that of a ninth-grade student. Write it right and simply.

Consult Appendix A in *PRW3e* to learn how to do a readability analysis of your writing. You'll probably use the Flesch or Gunning Method. Identify the method used, and show your calculations on the back of your report. Turn in the report on the due date.

The business of banking at FNB is based on <u>lending</u> and <u>borrowing</u>. Like any enterprise, FNB operations are based on <u>capital</u>. As with other banks, FNB uses very little of its capital in proportion to its total transactions. The purpose of <u>capital and reserve accounts</u> at FNB is to protect against losses on <u>loans</u> and <u>investments</u>. FNB is limited by law in the proportion of its capital it can lend to a single borrower.

Essential characteristics of banking at FNB are describable as a <u>balance sheet</u>. One side of the balance sheet shows FNB's primary <u>liabilities</u>, or its <u>capital</u>, including <u>reserves</u> and <u>deposits</u>. Deposits may be <u>demand</u> or <u>time</u>. They also may be <u>domestic</u> or <u>international</u>.

The other side of the balance sheet contains FNB's <u>assets</u>, which include <u>cash</u> that may be in the form of <u>credit balances</u> at other banks, <u>correspondent banks</u>, or <u>federal reserve banks</u>; <u>liquid assets</u> that can be <u>converted</u> quickly, such as <u>treasury bills</u>, <u>short-term</u> notes, and the like; <u>investments</u> or <u>securities</u>, many of which are medium- to long-term <u>government securities</u>, such as <u>state and municipal bonds</u>; <u>loans</u> to customers; and FNB's premises, furniture, fittings,

equipment and the like, all <u>written down</u> to nominal
levels.

FNB's balance sheet also shows <u>contingent liabili-
ties</u>, or <u>bills of exchange</u> endorsed by the bank.
These are exactly balanced with borrowers' obligations
to <u>indemnify</u> FNB. Like other banks its size or
larger, FNB uses <u>banker's acceptance</u>, which attaches
its name and reputation to a transaction and ensures
that the <u>paper</u> will be more readily <u>discounted</u>.

NATS 6 : 1

Ms. Louise Cooper teaches health education to seniors at Serene High
School. She's assembling information for her course from many
sources, including information about emergency medicine and car-
diopulmonary resuscitation (CPR). Because NATS is headquartered in
Serene, she has asked you to write a one-page, typed or word-processed, double-spaced summary she can duplicate and give to her
students. A quick search in the files turns up the following copy. You
check it and find it is written at about the 17th grade level, so you
know it must be rewritten completely for her use. Because it will be
given to high school seniors, you decide to rewrite it at the 10th grade
level. Consult Appendix A in *PRW3e* for ways to do readability analy-
ses of your writing. You'll probably use the Gunning or Flesch
Method. Show the method used and your calculations on the back of
your report. Pay particular attention to the underlined jargon words
below. You must know what these words mean before you rewrite the
material. Then rewrite the material and turn it in on the due date.

<u>Emergency medicine</u> continues to grow. But it did not
become a <u>board-certified speciality</u> until 1979.
Emergency medicine seeks to prevent and treat <u>trauma</u>
of all types. About 80,000,000 people were treated in
1990 for trauma in the <u>emergency rooms</u> of about 5,400
hospitals in the United States. This treatment used

the services of about 15,000 <u>emergency medicine physicians</u>; 300,000 <u>emergency medicine technicians</u>; 30,000 <u>intermediate emergency medical technicians</u>; 40,000 <u>paramedics</u>; 80,000 <u>emergency room nurses;</u> and about 90 <u>hospital-based helicopter transport systems</u>.

An important treatment procedure used with many trauma patients is <u>cardiopulmonary resuscitation</u> (CPR). This treatment evolved when <u>artificial ventilation</u> was combined with the older technique of <u>chest compression</u>, sometimes called <u>closed chest cardiac massage</u>. Medical researchers don't agree on what makes CPR a viable emergency treatment in some situations. But they continue to search for more effective methods, such as changing the relationship of <u>ventilations</u> to <u>compressions</u> or adding intermittent <u>abdominal counterpulsations</u>, but improvements have yet to change the basic CPR guidelines in use since the 1960s.

CPR is a temporary measure used until <u>external cardiac defibrillation</u> can be given. The quicker <u>defibrillation</u> is provided, the more successful the result. <u>Automatic defibrillators</u> are becoming more common, and even some ambulance services now are equipped with these devices. Some forecasters say automatic defibrillators may become as common as fire extinguishers in public gathering places.

NCCC 6 : 1

Ms. Backe finishes going through the morning's mail and asks you to come to her office as soon as possible. You save and close the word-processing file you're working on and enter her office. She hands you a letter from Sully Trotter, for whom you've been working on a brochure. Attached to the letter is a second sheet of information.

"I want you to handle Sully's request, and I'll need it before you leave work today," Backe says. You read the letter and the information attached. Trotter's letter is complimentary of the overall concept of the brochure and design and most of its copy. But Sully points out that the clients and potential clients of NCCC services represent a broad range of educational levels. At least one parent in most client households has a college degree. Many others have some college. A few only have high school diplomas. The average number of years of school is 13 for the least-educated spouse in client and potential client households.

The letter says that NCCC believes strongly in the need for preenrollment evaluations of preschool children. NCCC also believes it is important that all parents of clients and potential clients understand completely what is involved in these evaluations. Sully notes that the copy section below is written at about the 17th grade level. "Although some of our clients can easily understand it, most can't," she says. "Please rewrite this section at about the 11th grade level. Surely, you have a writer at ProCom who can clean up this educationese."

As you prepare to rewrite this material, look hard at the underlined jargon words. Make sure you understand them fully before you start writing. Your rewrite must fit the space provided in the brochure's design. Plan on 225 to 250 words. Consult Appendix A in *PRW3e* for ways to test the level of your writing. When you finish, write on the back of your copy the name of the method used to check readability and show your calculations. Turn the rewrite in on the due date.

Most preschool children conceive of themselves and others in simple <u>evaluative</u>, <u>concrete</u> terms. They construct their realities in rigid "good" and "bad" zones. They react to the <u>interpersonal behavior</u> of others and events <u>egocentrically</u> as they <u>internalize</u>

how these behaviors and events may affect them. Because their life experiences are limited and they
often can't articulate their thoughts well,
preschoolers are somewhat trapped in the present and
must treat each situation as an isolated incident in
which the actions and beliefs of others are unpredict-
able.

They perceive of covert variables, such as emotion or
motive, as rudimentary, global and rigid. Their
evaluations of others are greatly biased by immediate
and observed events and behaviors, and they find it
difficult to relate one conceptual dimension to another. This makes it difficult for them to deal si-
multaneously with multiple cues or to integrate sequential or inconsistent information. Preschool children also may confuse the temporal and sequential
dimensions of events and they often mix wishful thinking with facts. They are inclined to dwell on events
that emphasize pleasures and sorrows, rather than on a
broader range of emotions.

A primary technique of evaluating preschool children
is to observe them while they engage in play. Special
attention is given to the characteristics of play,
such as its initiation, energy expended, manipulative
actions, tempo, body movements, tone, integration,
creativity and how children relate to other people

during play. Evaluators look for <u>behavioral evidence</u> regarding <u>persistence</u>, <u>orderliness</u>, <u>ingenuity</u>, <u>competitiveness</u>, <u>closure</u> and <u>intensity of play</u>.

NCCC believes preschool assessments are necessary to its success at grouping children according to <u>levels of development</u>.

TEI 6 : 1

Harry Culver, vice president for marketing at Tentative Electronics, Inc., has asked ProCom to provide some training materials for the TEI sales force. ProCom has been working on this project for some time, but there are still some problems to work out. One is that Culver wants his salespeople to better understand the theory behind how the Money Machine 2001 operates. He has asked TEI's chief engineer and primary designer of the Money Machine 2001, Dr. Ector Ellis, to write an explanation that could be used.

When Culver got the report, he passed it on to ProCom with the request to rewrite it in plain, simple terms. Your task is to rewrite the explanation. The TEI sales force has an average education level of 15. All have high school diplomas. Some have BBA degrees. One has an MS. Most have some college. Dr. Ellis's explanation is written at the 17th grade level. You must rewrite it at about the 12th grade level. As you do that, pay particular attention to the underlined jargon words. They're words meaningful to electrical engineers who deal in information theory and servo-mechanisms.

When you understand these terms, do a one-page information sheet that describes the theory behind how the Money Machine 2001 works. It should be typed or word-processed and double-spaced. Consult Appendix A in *PRW3e* to learn how to analyze the readability of what you write. You'll probably use the Flesch or Gunning Method. Write on the back of your report the method used and show your calculations. Turn in the report on the due date.

The theory behind TEI's Money Machine 2001 is fairly simple. As with any <u>automated system</u>, it has a large number of <u>action elements</u>, <u>sensors</u> and <u>control elements</u> combined in a series of <u>feedback loops</u>. All of these are under the control of a <u>complex computer program</u>, combined with sophisticated <u>decision-making equipment</u>. The design's sophistication is illustrated by the fact that when an action element does something, it may alter the actions of some or all other action elements.

Designing a system like the Money Machine 2001 depends on knowing each action element and its <u>interactions</u>, and <u>integrating</u> this information into the program so that proper <u>decision-making routines</u> are available when needed. One must also consider how the feedback loops behave, especially when they are part of a system with many <u>interacting elements</u>.

Simply stated, an <u>actuating signal</u> on the <u>input</u> of an action element produces an <u>output</u>. Part of this output may be a signal on the input to a feedback element. Output from the feedback element is sent to a <u>comparator</u>. The comparator gets a <u>reference input</u> from the <u>process program</u>. If these differ, a new <u>actuating signal</u> is generated. This new signal acts on the action element to produce a new output. This process continues until the feedback signal matches the reference input. A change in the reference input or output will, through feedback loops, drive the action element in a different direction.

A pitfall in automated systems is that feedback loops may be too slow to control the behavior of action elements. However, if feedback loops are too fast, then the system may <u>overcorrect</u> and begin to <u>oscillate</u>. If the feedback loops are properly timed, however, customers using the Money Machine 2001 can complete their transactions accurately and at their own speed.

Notes -

Quick-Study 7

Extract, Chapter 7, "Grammar, Spelling, Punctuation," *Public Relations Writing: Form & Style* 3e, Belmont, California: Wadsworth, 1991

S ome people believe you "should write like you talk." There's some merit in this belief because good writing sounds conversational. But this view is used sometimes as an excuse for breaking every known rule of good grammar. It may be true that rules are substitutes for thought, but there lies the great strength of rules. People will understand more quickly if you write by the rules. If you don't, most people may not stop to think about your meaning. They'll just direct their attention elsewhere.

You learned as a child that sentences are formed by arranging subjects, verbs and objects in that general order. And you also learned some punctuation marks serve as the traffic lights of grammar. You may get maimed or killed if you run a red light in your car. The meaning of what you write may suffer similar semantic harm if you violate grammar's common rules. It also is foolhardy to mix chemicals indiscriminately because they may blow you to smithereens. If you carelessly mix words and phrases, your writing may explode in your face. Good writers work hard to produce explosions of understanding, not misunderstanding.

Some writers fall into a trap if they try too hard to economize with words. Although tight writing is expected in public relations, it can lead to *ambiguity*. You leave out "that" or use "which" instead of "that." This is especially true if you favor "which" clauses. Ambiguity also creeps in when subjects and verbs don't agree, when you don't know whether something is singular or plural. Although "data" is the plural of "datum," current usage accepts "data" as plural or singular. Such plurals as "media" for "medium" are standard usage, but "medias" or "mediums" isn't. Therefore, the word *media* requires a plural verb; the word *medium*, a singular. Commas that set off phrases can also cause confusion. "Mary Marks, and other students, are going to class at 11 A.M." Just delete the set-off phrase and write: "Mary Marks is going to class at 11 A.M."

One *myth of grammar* is that the word "none" is less than one, so it must be singular. Dictionaries generally say none is plural. And that's the way most people use it when they talk. Look hard at the rules for the use of I and me. *Between* is the word that usually gets you into trouble. Use "between you and me." One rule says that you shouldn't split infinitives, and that's generally a good idea. But you may cause some confusion if you follow it blindly. Let the situation be your guide. Usually, you should avoid ending sentences with prepositions, but, like the rule on split infinitives, this is an influence from Latin purists who have handed it down over the centuries. If a sentence sounds better with a preposition at the end, write it that way.

Always keep a good grammar or language usage manual handy. But remember that such books are nothing more than collections of conventional practices. They can't answer every question. At best they may only suggest guidelines. And when you're writing messages for distribution through the mass media, you must conform to the style manuals those media use, despite what *your* manual says. Remember also that active voice is preferred, although passive may be better in some situations. Let circumstances dictate which one.

Spelling errors can quickly kill the effectiveness of otherwise good writing. Poor spelling casts doubt on your ideas. There is no dishonor in being a lousy speller. Dishonor comes from not recognizing the problem, and doing something about it. Consult an authoritative dictionary often. If you're writing on a word processor equipped with a spell-check program, use it. And be sensitive to word choices. The wrong word choice spelled correctly is still the wrong word. If your word processor has a grammar-check program, use it too, but don't expect much help from it if you are already a skilled writer.

EXERCISES

All Scenarios 7 : 1

ProCom has a style manual for its publications and promotional pieces. But when ProCom produces materials for a client, it uses the client's style. When it takes on a new client, ProCom's standard practice is to review the new client's style manual. If the client does not have one, ProCom studies the client's needs and recommends a particular style. Once the client agrees, ProCom employees faithfully follow that style. The problem confronting you now is that the client to which you are assigned—FNB, NCCC, TEI or NATS—does not have a style manual. Your assignment is to develop one.

This assignment requires you to consider a wide range of style issues. Most client style manuals are built on the Associated Press style manual, especially for clients that produce lots of materials for mass media distribution. Often an organization will have three style manuals. One is an internal organizational style manual that details precisely how people will be addressed in letters, memos and the like. Another is a manual used to produce consistency in company newsletters, employee magazines and the like. Yet another is the style used when producing news releases and other materials to be distributed to the mass media. Here are some suggestions to help you develop a style manual for the client.

First, construct a detailed list of style items specific to the client. This list would include such things as the proper spelling of the client's name, abbreviations, titles, acronyms and the like. Most style inconsistencies occur in these areas. Unless you identify these areas clearly, you can't do a good job of recommending an appropriate client style manual.

Second, get a copy of Thomas W. Lippman's article, "Why We Write It The Way We Do." This article appeared in *The Washington Post* (National Weekly Edition), March 27-April 2, 1989, p. 25. Your instructor can copy it from page 29 in the *Instructor's Manual* that accompanies *PRW3e*. Lippman reviews several thorny issues you must resolve as you consider problems of style relative to your client's needs.

Third, get a copy of the AP print and broadcast style manuals. Study carefully the contents of each section. Note what does not meet your client's needs.

Select one of the style manual types described above. Submit a style manual to the client (your instructor). It should be a typewritten or word-processed report that shows detailed style provisions that meet the client's needs.

Independent 7 : 1

The Chamber of Commerce in your hometown does not have a style manual. Construct one for it. Follow the instructions detailed above.

Quick-Study 8

Extract, Chapter 8, "Memos and Letters, Reports and Proposals," *Public Relations Writing: Form & Style* 3e, Belmont, California: Wadsworth, 1991

When you become a professional public relations writer, you'll probably find that you write more memos and letters than anything else. Even beginning writers write many of them. And you'll probably be surprised at how many reports and proposals you're expected to complete.

Organizations use *memos* mostly internally. Some companies have their own memo forms. You merely insert information in the right places. You must rely on your best judgment when memo forms are not used, but consult the heading style on p. 142 in *PRW3e*. Memos often have more visual cues than letters, such as numbered lists, indented sections and other formats.

One common memo writing trap is the failure to give enough context for content. Just because people work with you, don't assume they have the background needed to understand your memo. Don't be afraid to explain background, especially when writing to someone you don't know or who is in another department.

 A memo generally falls into one of six types. They are *bulletin, essay, informative, action, summary* and *file*. Review their descriptions in *PRW3e*, pp. 144-152. Personalize your memos. Pay attention to how they are distributed. If they are to be mailed, you may want to adopt a tone different from that of a memo to be posted.

Letters are used mostly for communication outside companies. They may have as many as six parts: *heading, salutation, body, close, signature* and *reference matter*. Letters are generally a little more formal in tone than memos. The situation and the relationship between the writer and addressee govern the tone.

Organizations use letters extensively for promotional purposes. A modest investment in a promotional letter may yield big returns. To be truly productive, promotional letters must interest receivers and be written clearly and simply. The more you expect of readers, the clearer you must be.

You'll likely be writing reports and proposals too. A *report* is simply a well-documented research paper that gives background material that explains a subject. A *proposal* is equally well documented, but it usually advocates a course of action. Both reports and proposals use footnotes, tables, charts and related materials, depending on the topic and situation. Recall how you prepared and wrote essays, themes and research papers and reports when you were in school. If you don't remember how to source and cite materials, get a good style manual and keep it by your side.

Although reports and proposals have different purposes, they usually have some things in common. Enclose a *cover letter* with each report or proposal. Address it to the person or group who will read the document. A cover letter briefly summarizes the content of the report or proposal. Use a *letter of transmittal* when the report or proposal was assigned by a person or group other than the recipient. A letter of transmittal defines who made the assignment, why it was assigned, and explains how the task was performed. It may also include a brief summary.

The *front matter* of a report or proposal includes such things as a title page, table of contents, and so on—much like the pages that precede the first chapter in a book. A *synopsis* page precedes the first page of the body of the report. Such a page is sometimes called an *abstract*, but the preferred label in the business world is *executive summary*. It is usually just one page, never more than two. It summarizes the highlights of the report or proposal. It must be complete enough that someone won't have to read the whole document to know what it is about.

The *body* of the report or proposal has three major elements: *introduction*, *body* and *conclusions*. The introduction reviews the problem and how it was studied. A thesis statement or hypothesis *provides a context for the body*. Anything not related to the central idea should be excluded from the body. Conclusions must be derived logically from the material in the body. Recommendations can follow conclusions, when appropriate.

Reports and proposals generally include *references*. These document the sources used to explain information not known commonly by those who read and evaluate reports or proposals. Always use footnotes or endnotes. And remember to include a complete *bibliography* of all information surveyed, including information consulted but not used.

An *appendix* contains detailed information important to the report or proposal but whose insertion in the body would disrupt reading. If you are writing to or in a specialized field, use as little jargon as possible in your document. Expect to rewrite your report or proposal several times before you write it right.

EXERCISES

FNB 8 : 1

A bank employee has suggested that First National Bank put ATMs on the State University campus. FNB management tells ProCom to follow up on the idea, and you are asked to write a proposal that management can submit to the university. Write a cover letter to go with the proposal to the university. Also write a short memo to management that explains the strategic idea behind the proposal. Spell out clearly the benefits to the university if ATMs are installed on campus. This memo is especially important to the members of the management team who will negotiate with Dr. Lott and other university leaders.

NATS 8 : 1

Realizing that many accident victims are even more seriously injured at the accident scene by amateurish efforts to administer first aid, you suggest that ProCom produce for NATS a first-aid booklet quite unlike other first-aid booklets. Your booklet will not only visually illustrate the right way to do things but also the wrong way. Not only is the wrong way clearly illustrated, but the booklet also shows the sometimes-dire consequences of the incorrect administering of first aid. Write a memo to ProCom management that summarizes your idea. After some discussions with you, ProCom management has floated the idea with NATS. NATS management likes it, and has given its approval for a rough draft of a few pages for review. Because it was your idea, ProCom assigns you the task of writing the draft. As it is to be only part of a completed booklet, you elect to do a representative section on a topic like CPR, emergency treatment of shock or severe burns or another emergency procedure. Create no more than four pages for this section of the booklet, including illustrations. When this section is complete, write a cover letter to NATS about what you want to present in the rest of the booklet. To do this assignment well, you'll need to review first-aid procedures. Consult the library.

NCCC 8 : 1

Although Dr. T. A. Lott, president of State University, severed ties with ProCom when the scholarship scandal broke regarding Ms. Melody Hanzout, the relationship resumed when Dr. Lott called George Schuss, president of NCCC, and suggested NCCC establish a child-care center on campus to serve the needs of students, staff and faculty. Schuss told Lott that NCCC only considers proposals approved first by its agency, ProCom. He further suggested to Lott that the university work with ProCom to develop a proposal for such a venture. That's when Dr. Lott returned to ProCom. Ensuing discussions with Dr. Lott led to the conclusion that the proposal should recommend that NCCC develop a pilot program on campus. If the venture proved successful, it could be a model to market similar NCCC programs on campuses nationwide. You are assigned to write the proposal from Lott to Schuss, as well as a cover letter.

TEI 8 : 1

TEI is watching carefully FNB's proposal to put ATMs on the State University campus. Oscar House has been concerned lately about the poor financial conditions in which TEI is trying to market ATMs. Although House is aware that a few campuses have ATMs, he's toying with the idea of developing a marketing strategy to market ATMs directly to campuses nationwide, in cooperation with local banks. House is considering the benefits of proposing a joint venture to FNB regarding the installation of ATMs on the State University campus. He's prepared to sell an ATM to FNB at cost, and he'll provide the installation free of charge to the bank and the campus. All he wants is the full cooperation of the bank and the university in selecting the best site for an ATM. House has asked ProCom to write a proposal to that effect. You draw the assignment. The proposal will go first to FNB. Write a cover letter to Olan Gable. When FNB accepts the proposal, write a cover letter to Dr. Lott at State University.

Independent 8 : 1

Get a copy of the advertising rate card used by your university's newspaper. Also get a copy of the policies the newspaper uses in accepting and/or refusing advertising. Review these policies and the rate card. Write a proposal for a new (or revised) set of policies and rate card intended to make them clearer and more complete. Also write a cover letter to accompany your proposal.

Notes -

Quick-Study 9

Extract, Chapter 9, "Backgrounders and Position Papers," *Public Relations Writing: Form & Style* 3e, Belmont, California: Wadsworth, 1991

Backgrounders and *position papers* are especially important documents in public relations, but beginning writers seldom appreciate their true values. Backgrounders provide common information bases on topics. Position papers provide rationales for planned or completed actions.

Backgrounders have many uses. They provide source material for writers preparing ad copy, speeches, news releases, annual reports, newsletters, magazines and the like. Backgrounders go to reporters, media and to other interested parties. They also may give context to media kits. Company executives consult them extensively when they plan and execute programs.

The key to writing successful backgrounders is the quality of the research that supports them. Review Chapter 4 in *PRW3e*, pp. 58-88. The information you need for a backgrounder is probably available. Your job is to find it. Rarely is primary research needed. If it is, do it.

[handwritten: must do research]

Don't try to write a backgrounder until you know enough about the assigned topic. Begin with a declarative sentence that describes the backgrounder and why it is important. Begin writing the body of the document only when this sentence is perfected. Your backgrounder stresses history, trends, events, people, legislative actions and like matters relevant to the topic. Your task is to provide objective background and context for understanding the current scene. Then describe the current scene thoroughly.

Backgrounders often end with a presentation of the implications or consequences of taking one direction or action over others. Keep your *opinions* to yourself. Avoid editorializing. Let facts speak for themselves. Document everything you write. Cite the source for every fact that is uncommon knowledge to your readers. You must be a good scholar to do good backgrounders.

The term *position paper* describes what it is. It says, "This is where we stand on this matter." And it provides a rationale for that position. Like backgrounders, position papers require research. If you have good, current backgrounders, your research is done. You simply review the relevant backgrounders before working out a position. If you find holes in the information, do more research.

Write a declarative sentence stating your position. If you can't immediately reduce the position to a simple sentence, keep trying. Avoid qualifying clauses and phrases. Keep it simple. Take a position only after weighing related facts and issues. Build your paper on selected facts. Remember that a position paper should not recite history in detail. Nor should it be burdened with too many facts, like long lists of numbers, names, and the like. That kind of information is for backgrounders.

Focus on the most important facts supporting your point of view. Advocate your position strongly, but fairly. Use footnotes or endnotes to cite the sources on which your position is based, although these are rarely as extensive in position papers as in backgrounders. Don't ignore other positions. You'll gain more supporters if you show accurately other points of view. That's because many of your readers will be no more than neutral toward your position. Some will be opposed to it. Both groups are naturally skeptical. If you do not show opposing points of view, even your supporters may have second thoughts about the position you advocate.

Remember your audience. Position papers are seldom written to a single audience. They may be used with many audiences, which makes writing an acceptable position paper more difficult than a backgrounder. The latter deals with facts. The former deals with opinion. Opinions are always debatable. Facts are less so. A good bibliography is always helpful.

Formats for each document vary. Backgrounders and position papers used internally often are simply typed and copied for limited distribution. If used outside the company, they may be typeset and printed for a better look. They are often three-hole punched so they can go into binders from which older versions have been discarded. Both documents use charts, graphs and tables. Always put these materials close to the narrative to which they apply.

EXERCISES

FNB 9 : 1

As an active member of the ProCom staff, you are aware of the recent trend toward bank mergers that produces megabanks. For example, the merger of NCNB (North Carolina National Bank) with C&S, which had only recently merged with Sovereign, produced Nation's Bank, one of the country's largest banks, behind only Citicorp and Chemical (a merger of what was Chemical Bank of New York and Morgan Bank).

Such developments as these tend to concentrate more power in the hands of fewer people. And some analysts say that although this trend may produce greater economic efficiencies, personal banking services may suffer creeping paralysis because of increased size.

But perhaps size itself is not so much an issue as is the remoteness of policy-makers from customers. A decision on a loan application, for example, may not be made by the management team at the local bank but by a team at corporate headquarters, thus delaying the decision-making process. That this outcome is inevitable is debatable.

FNB firmly believes it is inevitable. In fact, FNB management has asked ProCom to produce a well-developed position paper that argues that the best customer services will continue to come from smaller, local or regional banks, not megabanks. You draw this assignment, so the first thing you do is spend a good bit of time in the library reviewing books and journals on banking, especially those whose focus is customer service. When the proposal is complete, send it, along with a cover letter, to Olan Gable.

TEI 9 : 1

Some people fear using ATMs because they have heard about robberies at ATM sites. The "common knowledge" (not actually a rumor) is that potential robbers sometimes lurk near ATMs, waiting for customers to withdraw cash so they can take it from them. Although customer safety at ATM sites is beyond TEI's direct influence, it represents a legitimate concern. Banks may defer buying ATMs because they fear not enough customers will use them. If use is minimal, the purchase price can't be defended to boards of directors.

So TEI wants a thorough backgrounder done on customer safety at ATM sites. You draw the assignment. You'll need to review a wide range of materials in the library about customer safety of ATMs nationwide. Do your research well. When you have the backgrounder done, send it to TEI, along with a cover letter to Carla Chase.

NATS 9 : 1

One of NATS's beliefs is that emergency medicine centers are clogged with people who should not be there. Some are there because they have headaches or backaches or similar ailments that they can't bring under control with aspirin or Tylenol. And they don't want to wait to see their own physicians the next day. Others are there because of accidents that could have been easily prevented. For example, poisonous chemicals may be stored carelessly so they are easily accessible to children. Or a boiling pot is left unattended while someone answers a phone call in the next room. A curious child pulls the pot off the stove and gets burned severely.

NATS wants to develop a program that will educate and sensitize people to the need to practice good home and driving safety as a way of reducing the demand on emergency medicine centers. Before launching such a campaign, NATS has asked ProCom to develop a position paper that clearly defines the NATS position. ProCom assigns this task to you.

You'll need to do a good bit of library research about the state of emergency medicine. One issue you must address is the problem of poor people who depend on emergency rooms for their total health care because they can't afford regular physicians. When you finish the position paper, write a cover letter to Arty Hart.

NCCC 9 : 1

Nearly every business must be concerned with anything that affects the "bottom line," but particularly so with employees. If employees are preoccupied with the cost and quality of the care their children receive while they (the parents) are at work, employees aren't as productive as they might be. Some companies now argue that it is in the interest of their bottom lines to provide on-site, employer-subsidized child care for their employees' children. Employees pay only a nominal share of the cost. Some companies even provide these services for free.

George Schuss and Sully Trotter see this trend as one that can benefit NCCC. They want to sell companies on the idea of developmental child-care centers. Although child-care centers must tend to the physical needs of children, NCCC believes these centers also should have clearly focused developmental roles. That's a point of view business has not fully accepted.

Schuss and Trotter asked ProCom to prepare a well-researched position paper that defines the benefits of developmental child-care centers. They'll use this position paper to develop a marketing program to companies nationwide, touting NCCC as a vendor capable of providing these services on site. ProCom assigns this task to you.

You'll need to do a good bit of research on developmental child care. When you write the position paper, relate your findings to the benefits that can accrue to companies that use this approach to child care. When you finish, provide a cover letter from ProCom to Schuss and Trotter.

Independent 9 : 1

Choose an issue that is currently of concern on your campus. Do a thorough backgrounder on it. Then consider what you think about the issue and write a report that details your position. Write a cover letter for both documents, addressed to your professor.

Notes -

Quick-Study 10

Extract, Chapter 10, "News Releases for Print Media," *Public Relations Writing: Form & Style* 3e, Belmont, California: Wadsworth, 1991

Many *news releases* for print media aren't used because they have no genuine news-worthiness. The attitude of managers in the print media is that if you want to see a puff piece in print, buy an ad. You must know what constitutes news for the media. And you must know your company well enough to recognize news when you see it.

The lead sentence or paragraph of a news release must be short. And it should have a local angle, not only to catch the editor's eye but also to interest readers. Develop the second paragraph and body of the story with concise sentences and precise facts about the *who, what, when, where, how* and *why*. Often the *why* governs whether a story gets printed. It also influences the type of play your release gets; that is, whether it gets featured treatment or is cut and buried in the back pages.

You'll be more successful at writing news releases if you play the role of a reporter for the newspaper or magazine for which the release is intended. The difference is that you can create quotes to fit your release. Always clear these quotes with the persons being quoted. That's a luxury reporters don't have.

News releases must be simple, clear and direct in style. Always consult and follow the *AP Stylebook*. Some media have their own styles. Know these variations on the AP style, and use them.

Sometimes you'll give news tips to the media instead of writing news releases. If these tips provoke interest among editors, reporters will be assigned to write the stories. You'll be asked to help them with facts, site visits, interviews and the like. Stories written by media reporters usually get printed. The risk here is that reporters may say something about your company you don't want to see in print.

The focus of news releases varies with each situation. Some merely state information. Others relate special events or explain responses to events. Still others contain real spot news or feature materials, or are reactions to bad news.

Some material won't work as a straight news release, yet it may be important enough to appear in other forms, as a good guest column or as a brief in a local column. Ask editors about this before you write, and then use a writing style adapted to the column. Or write the piece as a letter to the editor. Being alert to these outlets will get a lot more exposure for your company. Don't force material into a news release if it does not fit the format.

For any news release, confirm that facts, spelling and grammar are correct. Expect your releases to be edited. If they appear with only nominal changes, that's a good sign you're doing things right. If they're edited heavily, you aren't doing your job well. Compare what appears in print with what you sent. Learn how to correct your mistakes by noting what professional editors do with your copy. When releases don't appear, this probably means you don't understand what is news. Compare releases not used to ones that are. You can sharpen your sense of news values from such a study.

Photographs, line art or schematics or other matter or tables should also be sent with news releases if this art adds interest to or explains content. Always provide complete captions; include names and titles of all people shown. Sometimes photos or other art, such as charts, with captions are run as "wild art." Most editors search daily for art to dress up their pages. Help them out.

Because many media won't run your releases for lack of interest or space, be selective about where you send them and to whom. Address releases to people by names and titles, and be sure you know these people. If the content of a news release is best suited for the business section, send it to the business editor. Send it to the person who writes the column if you want the information to appear as a brief. If you send the same release to competing media in the same market, you'll make enemies of both. Write separate releases, each crafted individually. You'll get more support if you follow that policy.

Some media prefer to have news releases fed directly into their electronic systems. It's your business to know that and what those systems are like. Tailor your format to those needs. Be sure your software is compatible with theirs. If that means you use several different software programs, do it. Don't balk. But before you send any news release, test it against the checklist in *PRW3e*, p. 207. If you answer no to any of those questions, correct the problem.

EXERCISES

FNB 10 : 1

TEI's proposal, as described in Assignment 8:1, to FNB for a joint venture brought quick approval from the bank. Representatives from the bank and TEI soon contacted the president of State University and finally got his reluctant support.

Approval came only after FNB agreed to pay the university a 10 percent commission on each campus ATM transaction fee collected. TEI offered to sell its Money Machine 2001 to FNB at 20 percent below cost, not at cost as was originally proposed. This encouraged FNB to yield to the university's insistence on some income from the venture.

So the first ATM on the State University campus is being installed now. It will be ready for business on Monday of next week. Although FNB leaders are excited about the deal cut with TEI, they aren't happy about having to pay a commission to the university.

What is needed now are news releases about the convenience of having an ATM on the campus. You are assigned to write the releases. Do one each for the *Clarion*, FNB's corporate publication, the alumni magazine at State University and another for the state's banking magazine. Be sure to tailor your releases to the audiences of these media.

Because it is a release from FNB, you'll likely give FNB the most prominent treatment, although FNB certainly wants credit given to TEI for its cooperation in this venture. You might note that the fee paid to State University will go into the general scholarship fund at the university, that the TEI unit being installed is the Money Machine 2001, and that it is being installed in the lobby of the student center.

Your releases might also point out that if ATM use meets expectations, others may be installed. Potential sites include the student post office, main cafeteria and the sports complex. The primary purpose is to make cash more easily available to students, staff and faculty.

TEI 10 : 1

Because TEI's Money Machine 2001 is being installed now on the State University campus and will be ready for business next Monday, TEI wants ProCom to produce some news releases about it. ProCom assigns you this task. Do a release each for the *Clarion*, TEI's corporate publication, the state banking journal and one for *American Banker*.

Although TEI leaders are pleased to see their Money Machine 2001 in use on campus, they feel like they've been ill used by FNB's greed. It became clear that FNB leaders were ready to walk away from negotiations because of Lott's insistence that FNB pay a commission to the university. Only when TEI lowered the cost to FNB was a deal struck.

One reason TEI made its initial proposal to FNB was that it wanted an ATM unit on a campus that could be monitored for usage patterns. Chase suspects that campus usage patterns may differ a little from those in the general community.

If that is true, Chase intends to analyze those patterns with a view to designing an ATM more closely aligned with campus uses. Although TEI ATMs are in use on a few other campuses, the proximity to State University makes this one an ideal study site. And FNB has promised full cooperation in sharing usage data with TEI.

NATS 10 : 1

In Assignment 9:1, you did sample copy for a "different" first-aid booklet. Since then, NATS has approved the concept and you've finished the brochure. It is now in production and will be ready for distribution in about a week. NATS has asked ProCom to prepare a news release on the new brochure. Because you know the brochure's purposes and content better than anyone else at Pro-Com, the news release assignment is given to you. NATS wants a release each to the *Associated Press* (as this brochure is expected to be distributed nationally), the *Clarion* and the state medical and nursing association publications. Also do a release for the NATS newsletter.

NCCC 10 : 1

The position paper in Assignment 9:1 was used as the basis for an NCCC proposal to State University for a model developmental child-care center. A contract was completed after lengthy negotiations. Among others, the contract has these provisions:

1. NCCC will construct its own facility on land provided by the University in a 99-year lease at $1 annually. If NCCC builds its facility and begins operations on the campus, ownership of the

structure reverts to State University if NCCC decides to abandon the program for any reason. Abandonment also breaks the lease.

2. Client priorities are:

   A. Children of graduate students will be given first priority. Although the university will underwrite 25 percent of the costs for all children of graduate students, it will underwrite 75 percent of the costs for children of graduate teaching or research assistants.

   B. Children of undergraduate students have second priority. The university will underwrite 10 percent of the costs for children of all undergraduate students, but undergraduate lab assistants are underwritten at 25 percent.

   C. Children of hourly and professional staff members get third priority, and the university will underwrite their costs by 10 percent. Children of full-time employees earning less than $20,000 annually will be underwritten at 25%.

   D. Children of tenured faculty members get fourth priority, and the university underwrites their costs by 10 percent. Faculty members with the rank of instructor or assistant professor on the tenure-track will be underwritten at 25 percent.

   E. Children of townspeople will get fifth priority. There is no subsidy for these clients.

3. NCCC will employ at least eight faculty members at the University child-care center. These faculty members are specialists in clinical psychology and child development. Their academic homes are in the Department of Psychology and the School of Education at State University. This arrangement frees substantial budgeted funds the university can then use to cover the costs of developmental child care subsidies.

Ground breaking for the NCCC center is scheduled for Friday of next week. Construction begins the following Monday. The center will be fully operational by the beginning of the next academic year.

The University's public relations office would ordinarily do a news release on this project, but that office has agreed to let ProCom do the release for NCCC. State University's PR office has pledged full cooperation regarding background materials. However, it wants to see a draft of the release before it is distributed to the media.

Because you've worked closely with NCCC on other projects, ProCom assigns the writing of the news release to you. What is needed is a release each for the *Clarion*, the *Associated Press* (state wire), the university's alumni magazine and internal newsletter and NCCC's newsletter.

Independent 10 : 1

Get the results of the most recent national survey of the attitudes of new college students (first year students) and corresponding information about students at your university. Gallup, Roper, Harris and other pollsters do these studies routinely for some clients. The information often finds its way into the mass media.

Search such sources as the *New York Times Index* and *Reader's Guide to Periodical Literature* until you find the data you need. Go to a reference librarian if you run into trouble. For data at your own university, look first to the Office of Institutional Research. If there isn't an office with that or a similar title, inquire at the university's public relations office. Nearly every campus does research of this type. Study the two sets of data for similarities and differences. Do a news release for the student newspaper about the differences you find.

Notes -

Quick-Study 11

Extract, Chapter 11, "Broadcast Writing: News and Features," *Public Relations Writing: Form & Style* 3e, Belmont, California: Wadsworth, 1991

J ournalistic concerns for news values, factual accuracy, spelling and grammatical correctness apply as much to broadcast writing as to print. But sights and sounds drive broadcast writing. And special events are most probable, except for crises, to have the sights and sounds that get the most broadcast coverage, especially television coverage. So pay special attention to events that can lead to air time.

Much of your success at broadcast writing will depend on how well you prepare fact sheets that broadcasters can use. Supply a brief news release in broadcast style, although it may not get used as sent. Send along the print version, which is usually much longer, as information. Improve coverage by providing a segment of video- or audiotape.

If broadcasters cover a story on site, anticipate their needs for electrical power, staging areas, props and the like. Do everything you can to make their coverage as easy and as successful as possible. Use your own equipment to shoot or record the same event. This tactic provides good backup if their equipment fails. You also have an instant record of what happened at the event, which may be especially important in crises, or in ongoing controversial stories. And remember to post someone in a central area to answer broadcaster's questions and to provide information on demand.

You can call a news conference when someone from the company needs to interact with the media, or to announce a major development. Prepare for these events by writing or assembling fact sheets, backgrounders and position papers. These materials go into media kits along with broadcast and print news releases (the latter are for information only). Always cover your news conference as though you are a working member of the press. That not only helps you to see what happens from the media's points of view, it also lets you spot weaknesses in your preparation.

Instead of writing broadcast news releases, you may write minidocs (minidocumentaries). Minidocs are short, related stories in series, a format sometimes favored when a story is complex and time is not critical. A minidoc is usually written as a large, single script, and then broken into segments for airing in order. Some companies do a great many minidocs, but most don't. You are more likely to help a station's broadcast writers on assignment than to do a minidoc yourself.

Broadcast writing style is conversational. It uses active voice extensively. Broadcast writing also has two audiences. One is the announcer or other person who reads the copy aloud. The other audience is listeners or viewers. The physical appearance of the copy helps announcers. Copy's structure helps listeners or viewers. Broadcast leads seldom contain all the news elements seen in print news releases.

If you provide tape, radio places premiums on actualities (human voices and natural sounds of events or situations), but television prizes video with sound. Attach complete scripts to all audio- and video-tapes. A news release that coincides with the tapes also helps broadcast news editors as they prepare newscasts.

Broadcast news stories are rewritten several times daily. That's why most stations want more information than is in your audio or video tapes and scripts. It helps them dig for a new angle to freshen a story already aired several times. This is especially important to remember when you're dealing with crisis situations. Feed new information via phone or FAX to stations as quickly as you can verify its accuracy.

Talk-show appearances can't be scripted in the strictest sense. Your role is to provide biographical and background materials. Sometimes the host or a station staff member will provide a sample list of questions that may be discussed. This list speeds up and focuses your preparation of appropriate background materials. But sometimes you only know the general topic, so the material you write or assemble must be more extensive. In both cases, you must rehearse the person who will be interviewed. Play the role of interviewer and be a devil's advocate. Never let the interviewee get surprised by questions you didn't expect.

EXERCISES

All Scenarios and Independent 11 : 1

Do broadcast versions of the assignment described in 10:1. Do one for local television and one each for two different (your choice) radio stations in Serene. For the television release, turn in a production script that uses voiceover (VO) and film or video actualities. For radio, turn in a production script that uses VO and audio actualities. Be sure your scripts are clearly marked as to VO and actualities.

Notes -

Quick-Study 12

Extract, Chapter 12, "Writing Advertising Copy," *Public Relations Writing: Form & Style* 3e, Belmont, California: Wadsworth, 1991

You'll write a lot of advertising copy, but rarely for commercial products or services. Your efforts will focus on "idea" ads, sometimes called *advertorials*, if for print media, or *infomercials*, if for broadcast. You'll also write some *institutional, identity* or *corporate image* ads. But you'll write more *PSAs* than any other type of ad. PSA stands for a *public service ad* in print or a *public service announcement* in broadcast. The media run PSAs free as a public service on a space- or time-available basis. Review the content of Examples 1-10 in Chapter 12, *PRW3e*.

Advertising copy is persuasive. It asks people to accept an idea, take a position, buy a product or use a service. Advertising appeals are vital to effective persuasion. Appeals may be *rational, emotional* or a *combination* of the two. Rational appeals tug at the head and emotional appeals tug at the heart. Combination appeals begin with emotion to arouse attention and interest, switch in the body of the copy to a rational approach intended to provide reason-why information and end with a final appeal to the heart.

Appeals are also important when positioning your point of view. A road bond program positioned as a "safety" issue may get more support than if positioned merely as a "better roads" issue. An audience pays attention and responds positively to your messages for its own reasons, not yours. If the appeal you select is unimportant to your audience, your ads will be ineffective.

Basic guidelines for writing advertising copy include:

1. Know the purpose of your ads.

2. Know the objective facts about the topic.

3. Know what is important to your audience. If what you want is unimportant to your audience, reconcile the differences.

4. Know which media your audience pays attention to, and package your message in the right formats for those media.

5. Be original and creative in how you tell your story. Avoid triteness, mundaneness, cuteness and cleverness.

6. Think verbally and visually as you write. Use vivid words and illustrate them with evocative art, scenes, motion and/or sounds.

7. Use simple words, phrases and grammatical structures.

8. Repeat the central idea at least three times in each message, although it need not be repeated verbatim.

9. Expect to repeat the message several times before a threshold of effects (enough exposures to a message for it to begin to register with the receiver) is reached.

Decide whether your primary purpose is to *inform* or *persuade*. If to inform, your copy probably will be information-intensive. If to persuade, you'll use less information, but select it carefully to support your point of view.

Good copywriting follows four basic steps. Although these steps are most easily recognized in print messages, they apply equally to broadcast and film.

1. Getting an audience's *attention* is the first step. Provocative headlines and visuals can achieve this goal. Headlines that promise a benefit get the most attention.

2. *Interest* is piqued by the headline and the first sentence or paragraph of the copy by appealing to the audience's self-interest. Only if self-interest is aroused can you transfer it to interest in what you advocate.

3. The body of the copy should heighten *desire* for and *credibility* in what you advocate by supporting claims made or benefits promised. It establishes associations between facts and ideas about them.

4. The final step is to invite *action.* Effective ads always call for specific action, such as to support the United Way, to volunteer with the local literacy program or a myriad of others.

Simple words, phrases and grammatical structures are also hallmarks of good ad copy.

These same principles apply to writing copy for direct mail, mail-order and unmailed direct advertising and to all sales promotion materials. Creating effective outdoor ads may be the sternest measure of your skills as a copywriter. For an outdoor ad, you can't use more than about eight words of copy, including the client's name. You will find that especially challenging.

Preciseness, conciseness and clear style are hallmarks of broadcast and film copywriting. Such copywriting must be simple, direct and provocative. It should be conversational in tone so it sounds personal. Avoid generalities, exaggerations, slang and jargon.

A slice-of-life (SOL) technique is often favored because it easily portrays problems audiences can identify with and offers solutions to them. Jingles and humor are usually highly memorable. However, both can grow stale quickly. Heavy-handed humor can backfire. If you use humor, never poke fun at your audience.

EXERCISES

FNB 12 : 1

Some time ago FNB's management team reviewed your position paper on the impact of bank mergers on customer services. In fact, your position paper arguing that the best customer service will still come from smaller banks, not megabanks (Assignment 9:1) has been debated extensively at two different meetings of the board of directors. These debates were not centered on the rightness of the position advocated, but rather on what FNB could do about it.

Some directors seem to believe that FNB can't do anything because the big banks will just continue to gobble up smaller competitors. Other directors don't dispute that possibility, but believe FNB should meet the problem head-on in the Serene market. Their thinking is that branch banking and mergers make it possible for any bank, big or small, to compete with them in Serene. Every customer who carries a Visa or MasterCard from a bank outside Serene represents that competition.

Some directors also believe that some FNB customers have been lured away by special promotions and offers, such as a no-fee Visa or MasterCard for the first year or an all-expenses paid weekend in Las Vegas for jumbo CD deposits of $100,000. Directors also noted these come-ons actually cause customers to lose money.

Finally, FNB management has gotten approval from the board to launch a full-scale communication program intended to convey the idea that "FNB hasn't forgotten that it's your money." Brochures, advertorials and news releases will be used in the program. Several bank officers will do speaking engagements at such places as the Kiwanis Club and others. A five-minute audio-visual show (tape and 35mm color slides) will be produced to supplement these speeches. FNB will also make it available to public schools. ProCom assigns you the PSAs for the program.

Your instructions include:

1. Write a basic communications strategy for the campaign.

2. Write a basic creative strategy for the campaign's advertorial portion.

3. Although you'll do six or eight advertorials, ProCom only wants you to do three versions, one each for local newspaper, radio and television.

4. ProCom's creative team will review the two strategy statements and your model advertorials before they're shown to FNB staff.

TEI 12 : 1

The TEI management team and board of directors were impressed by the backgrounder you submitted in Assignment 9:1. Both groups had known intuitively that customer safety at ATMs was a problem, but they had not seen the documentation to support those beliefs. Of course, it is the bank's primary responsibility to install TEI's money machines in well-lighted areas.

Some banks *are* sensitive to the question of customer safety, especially banks whose ATM customers have been robbed, but most banks fear mounting a safety campaign because they're afraid it may drive customers away.

TEI still believes something should be done. It wants ProCom to design a campaign. TEI has warned ProCom in correspondence and in meetings that the ads must not alarm local bank managements or their customers.

This assignment is delicate, and some staff members at ProCom just simply can't handle it. So ProCom hands you the assignment because of the good work you did on the backgrounder. TEI also insists that its name not be used as part of the verbal message, but its ATM brand name can be shown in contextual visuals. A tagline may say something like "This message is brought to you in the interest of safe banking by (name of medium)" if you can get the media to agree to co-op the announcements.

Before you do the entire campaign, do one ad each for print, television and radio. These ads will be used as models for final program approval. Because these ads will be distributed nationally, the level of creativity and production values must be outstanding.

NATS 12 : 1

A continuing problem for NATS members is too much demand in many emergency rooms, especially in metropolitan areas. This demand leads to long hours for physicians and other staff people. It is aggravated by people who want emergency care when they really don't need it or they need care because they have not practiced good driving or home safety measures. These cases tax not only emergency care personnel, they deny proper care, in some cases, to those who need it most.

The position paper you prepared for NATS on preventable accidents has been reviewed carefully. The NATS leadership is now prepared to commit to an extensive, persuasive communication program intended to sensitize people to the problems of emergency medical care.

The program's basic purpose is to lighten the pressure on emergency care centers by helping people understand how to prevent the need for emergency care. Because of the quality of the position paper you did, NATS has requested that ProCom assign you this task. ProCom has agreed.

The first task you're assigned is to develop a communications strategy for the overall program. The next step is to develop a creative strategy that will focus the campaign. NATS wants to see newspaper, television and radio versions of a sample PSA before it gives full approval to the program.

NCCC 12 : 1

The NCCC leadership is excited about the early success of the child development center on the State University campus. Part of the excitement is because NCCC sees itself as contributing significantly to the education of students in the university's child development programs. It also feels that it is providing a living laboratory for faculty members, who can conduct their research on site.

Response from graduate students and faculty has been exceptionally good. They feel their children are being well handled by NCCC. Staff members report that children at the center are far better than average in terms of innate intelligence and most are developmentally from six months to better than two years ahead of their chronological ages. This finding has presented some significant new challenges to NCCC staff who appear to thrive on the challenge.

NCCC management believes it is time to "go public" with some image ads in a few prestigious journals and a "canned" one-time program for use on public television. NCCC has asked ProCom to assign you these tasks because of the excellent position paper you wrote in Assignment 9:1. But before NCCC authorizes the full program, it wants to see one sample print ad and a few pages of a proposed television script.

Independent 12 : 1

Write one each of a television and radio spot to be run locally. The focus of these spots is to promote the campus newspaper as a good place for certain types of businesses to advertise. You'll need to get as much information as possible about the local campus market and the readership of the campus newspaper. Be sure you understand the nature of buying behaviors and preferences of students at State University. Don't confuse them with the buying behaviors and preferences of faculty and staff.

All Scenarios and Independent 12 : 2

Read the direct mail ads in Examples 12:1, 12:2 and 12:3 that follow this assignment. Review the commentary that accompanies them. Your assignment is to produce a series of three print ads about yourself that evoke interest in your credentials as a prospective employee.

However, these ads should not replace a biographical summary. They are to be used only as a point of contact with potential employers and to get them interested in you. To do this assignment really well may be the most difficult assignment in this book. It is so difficult because many people often don't want to look closely at themselves. They're afraid of what they'll see. Avoid being trite, clever and cute.

Note these points about the examples:

1. The headlines are provocative, creative; they have stopping power.

2. The copy is direct, simple and displays the writer's creative ability.

3. The copy ties into the headline and leads the reader to an explanation of why it's better to hire Matt Fels than a yes man. The copy sets up the problem and offers a solution.

4. The logo asserts Matt Fels as "the why man."

Notes -

Example 12:1—Initial Idea and Use

Matt Fels positioned himself as "The why man" in these ads, presented as a series of three mailings at one-week intervals. Each ad was accompanied by a brief cover letter and a copy of his résumé. Invitations to interview came in quickly, and other people called to comment on his creativity. Just before he was ready to put the third piece in the mail, he landed a job as a copywriter with one of the three agencies for whom he most wanted to work.

Why is a hard word to say.

It's even hard to pronounce.
First you have to blow air through pursed lips, then open your mouth, and finish by pulling back the corners of your mouth. (Try it.)
Words like "no" are easier to say. Which may be one reason that people who say "why" first are hard to find.
That's why you need me. A "why" man.
English and history courses at TCU trained me to ask "why" to get to the heart of a problem. (You can't understand Macbeth—or the Alamo—if you don't ask why.) Advertising courses sharpened my copywriting, media planning and layout skills. And when I interned at The Old Spaghetti Warehouse, I combined the two disciplines. Sales increased 10 percent over companywide levels.
A "why" man can produce results for you. But don't just take my word for it. Contact me and ask me why.
Even though it may take a little effort.

Matt Fels. The why man.

Matthew B. Fels   4500 Brentwood Stair #2026   Ft.Worth TX 76103   817/429-9446 - Metro

Source: *Used with permission* of Matt Fels.

Example 12:1 (Continued)

The last thing you need is another yes man.

When you're running a lean operation, "yes" men (or women) can bog you down.

Same for "no" men.

They only tell you what you want to hear. Not what they actually think.

"Yes" men slow down the creative process. "No" men can stop it dead.

That's why you need me. Not a "yes" man or a "no" man, but a "why" man.

In my college and work experience, I've learned to work effectively in many different environments.

But I don't always tell people just what they expect to hear.

I listen first and ask questions that get people thinking objectively. And creatively.

It's this attitude that can help you produce ideas that achieve results.

If what you don't expect to hear is what you've been waiting to hear, contact me. But don't say yes—or no—just yet.

Matt Fels. The why man.

Matthew B. Fels   4500 Brentwood Stair #2026   Ft. Worth TX 76103   817/429-9446 - Metro

Example 12:1 (Continued)

Even the word Yes begins with a why.

Why this strategy? Why this target audience?
Why did idea A work better than idea B? Or, why
not consider this option?

Before you say yes, you have to say why.

Asking why can spot and strengthen a good idea.

Or smoke out a bad idea before it progresses too far.

That's why you need me. A "why" man.

The first thing I did at The Old Spaghetti
Warehouse was study the files. To determine
which strategies worked and which didn't.
And why.

Asking why helped me fine-tune Spaghetti
Warehouse advertising.

I revamped all existing ads to fit the company's
new campaign. Developed new promotions for
Father's Day and July 4, along with original ads.
And added PM drive radio to a print-heavy media
schedule.

Sales set three spot records and back-to-back
monthly records.

If you want more advertising that makes clients
and customers say yes, start with a why. Contact
me at the address below.

Matthew B. Fels   4500 Brentwood Stair #2026   Ft. Worth TX 76103   817/429-9446 - Metro

Example 12:2—First Adaptation

When Matt Fels won an Addy (advertising's Oscar) for creativity his first year after graduating from college, he positioned himself as "The Addy man" in this mailer to friends and colleagues around the country. Tasteful self-promotion can pay handsome dividends, but you must have something to promote.

Fort Worth, February 18, 1984

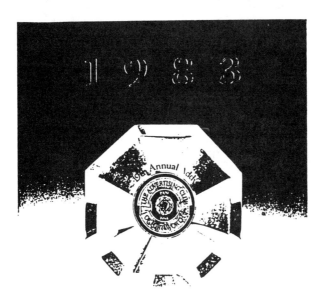

Example 12:3—Second Adaptation

When it was time to move on to bigger challenges, Fels sent an updated series of mailings patterned after the first one. He landed a senior copywriter position with a Dallas agency and now heads his own public relations and advertising firm. In both cases, the "why man" idea helped him get where he wanted to be.

When you need to be flexible, can you afford yes people?

Of course not. What you need is a why man.

Unlike "yes" people, who tell you only what they think you want to hear, a why man takes a true creative approach to problem solving. Asking the "why" questions that get to the meat of a situation.

Does the "why man" approach work? On accounts ranging from pizza to software, my copy has been part of a dozen gold and silver award winners. It's helped to obtain and build some great client relationships.

But the real strength of a why man is what happens between copy assignments. While working full-time as a copywriter, I've also managed to handle full media responsibilities, organize and conduct research, coach art staffers in desktop publishing and keep all agency computers running smoothly.

As you interview, you're going to talk with a lot of yes people. You may even hire a few. But when every campaign and every new-business presentation counts, you can't afford not to hire a why man.

Matt Fels. The why man.

Matthew Brian Fels   4125 Curzon   Fort Worth, Texas 76107   (817) 737-MATT

Source: *Used with permission* of Matt Fels.

Example 12:3 (Continued)

Why hire a copywriter when you can get a why man?

Here are two reasons: resourcefulness and profit.

Soon after one employer got its first PC, I thought, "Why not use microcomputers as a promotional medium?" In my spare time, I developed the first software-based marketing tool in the Southwest. A full year and a half before big advertisers like Ford picked up the idea.

Here's a more recent example. When I signed on with my current employer, I'd never spent more than a few half hours with a Macintosh. Within four months I became the fastest Mac production person in the house. And began showing co-workers how to make friends with the computer and get more done. A year later I was named director of technology, with responsibility over all the microcomputers in the agency.

If all you need is good ad copy, hire a copywriter. But if you're also looking for unthought-of ways to achieve unheard-of results, you need a why man. Contact me at the address below.

Matt Fels. The why man.

Matthew Brian Fels   4125 Curzon   Fort Worth, Texas 76107   (817) 737-MATT

Example 12:3 (Continued)

Why hire a media director when you can get a why man?

Here are two reasons: resourcefulness and profit.

Soon after one employer got its first PC, I thought, " Why not use microcomputers as a promotional medium?" In my spare time, I developed the first software-based marketing tool in the Southwest. A full year and a half before big advertisers like Ford picked up the idea.

Here ' s a more recent example. When I signed on with my current employer, I 'd never spent more than a few half hours with a Macintosh. Within four months I became the fastest Mac production person in the house. And began showing co-workers how to make friends with the computer and get more done. A year later I was director of technology, with responsibility over all the microcomputers in the agency.

If all you need are a few good media plans, hire a media director. If yo u ' re also looking for unthought-of ways to achieve unheard-of results, you need a why man. Contact me at the address below.

Matt Fels. The why man.

Matthew Brian Fels   4125 Curzon   Fort Worth, Texas 76107   (817) 737-MATT

Quick-Study 13

Extract, Chapter 13, "Crisis Communication," *Public Relations Writing: Form & Style* 3e, Belmont, California: Wadsworth, 1991

Effective writing in a crisis situation is more a test of your preparation for a crisis than it is of your writing skills. Remember only one rule: Be prepared. As a writer, you may have no direct responsibility for issues management, but you must know which issues may induce a crisis. And you must know what is the response plan if a situation reaches crisis levels. Only if prepared can you put into motion quickly and effectively a writing strategy.

Begin your preparation by imagining a worse-case scenario, even if it pales in comparison with what happens. Ask yourself "what if" questions. Only when you can give quick, good responses to those questions are you ready to begin your preparation. You must resolve two important issues. First, plan carefully how to sustain the flow of accurate and current routine information *inside* the organization. Second, plan carefully how to sustain communication with groups *outside* your organization, including the media.

Responsible firms develop crisis plans. These plans detail who will do what under which circumstances. Plans must be reviewed regularly and be in the hands of people who have primary response roles. A key tenet of most crisis plans is to name two spokespersons. One is responsible for communicating inside and the other outside an organization. The two spokespersons must rehearse regularly how to behave when a crisis strikes. Although factual accuracy is always prized, its value is never so great as in a crisis because that's when it is most difficult to verify.

Crisis plans usually name a crisis management team, including those named as inside and outside spokespersons. The team usually includes a few key officers whose energies and skills will be devoted to managing the crisis. Other officers continue operations as nearly normal as possible.

Your primary roles as a writer are to:

1. Create worst-case scenarios to which the crisis management team responds.

2. Rehearse the two spokespersons on how to interact with the media during a crisis.

3. Explain carefully why the same information must be given to audiences inside and outside the firm.

4. Rehearse other crisis team members who may interact with the media.

5. Have an adequate supply of documents nearby, such as facts sheets, position papers, backgrounders, biographies of key officers, pictures, maps, names, titles, addresses and phone numbers of key personnel (not just officers) and the like.

6. Anticipate where crisis command posts should be located and what facilities must be provided, such as phone lines, copy and FAX machines and the like.

7. Play the role of a reporter covering a crisis. Ask difficult questions. By listening carefully to answers, you can be ready to respond to real questions when the occasion arises.

8. Call press conferences only on an as-needed basis.

The quality of your organization's leadership makes your job easier or more difficult during crisis situations. If leaders are open and candid, your job is easy, although contending with a crisis tends to mask this value until after a crisis is over. It is easier for you to take charge of the situation by sharing information quickly and freely. And your organization will come out better in the long term. Faced with questions that may represent security or legal issues, you're free to say "I have the information, but I can't comment on that now."

Leaders who stonewall the media about a crisis make your role difficult. Reporters may try to trap you into revealing information. You and the organization may get pilloried because stonewalling is often interpreted as arrogant, not only by the media but also by audiences. If reporters are stonewalled, everything you say after a crisis will be viewed with suspicion, which can stretch a crisis beyond its normal span.

EXERCISES

FNB and TEI 13 : 1

A hacker got into the bank's electronic accounts system. The first evidence was some extraordinary errors in some accounts. For example, a college professor's bank statement showed a balance of $17,051.60 instead of $1,601.60. She didn't draw on it and immediately notified the bank. This oddity was traced to a TEI electronic transfer of $15,450 which showed up as $161. This TEI transfer was made to cover dividend checks to stockholders. Consequently, these checks began to bounce.

Meanwhile, an anonymous tip to a *Clarion* reporter claimed TEI had made an illegal contribution to State Representative P. N. Barrell. A *Clarion* investigation turned up a copy of Barrell's bank statement that showed TEI's contribution. The *Clarion* ran an extensive story about the contribution, which brought angry denials from TEI. But Barrell acknowledged that TEI money did turn up in his political campaign account, and he was effusive in his gratitude to TEI.

Several FNB customers have threatened legal action against the bank, as has TEI.

Meanwhile, a new and dangerous computer virus has invaded the FNB system and disrupted all electronic transactions. Because the virus is a new one, specialists are working frantically to produce counterprogramming to void the virus and restore data feared lost. Because several customers are likely to take legal action and because so many customers have been affected, FNB and TEI are perplexed as to what they should do. They've contacted ProCom for help in this crisis situation. ProCom has turned the problem over to you.

Write a report that explains exactly what FNB and TEI should do individually and collectively. Then write a news release for the *Clarion*, based on the actions that will be taken.

NATS 13 : 1

A national magazine published a cover story about emergency medical care that says it is the most expensive operation in hospitals. By inference, it implied emergency medical care is primarily responsible for consumers' mounting medical costs.

The same article also noted that emergency medical personnel are badly abused, working long hours under extraordinarily stressful circumstances. The same article pointed out cases where people died or were maimed because of mistakes made by emergency medical staff. The article's message is that emergency rooms are both extravagant and dangerous.

The story apparently also produced editorial interest in markets across the country. In fact, several stories in other print and broadcast media can be traced directly to that cover story. The NATS leadership is naturally distressed and wonders what it can do to meet this barrage of bad publicity.

NATS contacted ProCom and said, "Do something." After a quick huddle, ProCom assigns you the task. Write a plan of action, then follow through with a news release about the plan.

NCCC 13 : 1

A former Dallasite, who is now a popular recording artist, has just gone public with a personal story in which she says recent bouts with alcoholism have been traced by psychoanalysis to abuse she suffered as a child. She claims she had repressed memories of being sexually abused at the Stemmons Center (NCCC's first site) by a woman she can only vaguely remember as Ms. Jones. She says the abuse went on for about three years until her mother, a single working parent, put her in a different child-care center closer to her new home.

Although she has not told this story before, it is getting wide play in the media because of her fame as a rhythm and blues singer. Within two days after this story broke, parents pulled 16 children from enrollment at the Stemmons location. Other NCCC centers report some attrition, but nothing much beyond normal turnover.

Late this afternoon, three other adults came forward to say they were similarly abused by Ms. Jones when they were also clients at the Stemmons Center. NCCC management, immediately after the story broke, searched employment records, and issued a news release that said no one by the name of Jones (or by any name similar to it) had ever worked at the Stemmons location.

NCCC did not deny the story, only that a person by that name had never worked at the Center. NCCC promised to search employment records again. Later that evening NCCC told police it had found a record showing that an Evelyn Jossey had worked at the Stemmons facility for a period of four years in the mid-1970s, but that nothing in her record indicated anything irregular.

NCCC leadership is painfully aware of similar stories at other child-care centers in recent years, but it is unprepared to deal with the crisis. It called ProCom for help. ProCom passes the assignment to you. Thoroughly analyze the situation and work out a plan of action. Then write a news release that explains the plan.

Independent 13 : 1

A national publication has ranked all universities, based on the quality of education and the treatment students get. Your university is ranked in the lowest percentile. The admissions officer has asked ProCom to help construct a student perspective on this claim. The publication making the claim is often used by parents and students as they begin searching for a campus home.

It is important for your university to provide clear, documentable information about the campus and its education and treatment of students. This assignment has priority because the admissions office has already received calls about the story, although no enrollments have been cancelled. What plan of action do you recommend in this situation? Once you've developed a basic plan, write a news release about it for the campus newspaper.

Notes -

Quick-Study 14

Extract, Chapter 14, "Magazines and Employee Publications," *Public Relations Writing: Form & Style* 3e, Belmont, California: Wadsworth, 1991

D oing a feature for a magazine or an employee publication is probably one of the most enjoyable writing jobs in public relations. But not all writers handle feature materials well. They sometimes get so involved in the corporate culture that their stores fall flat because they have lost touch with their audiences. So the first rule about this type of writing is not only to know your audience, but to stay tuned into what interests it most, and why.

Finding story ideas is usually not difficult, but evaluating them may be. A key question is: Is the audience interested in this idea? A practical problem sometimes arises when you know a story is interesting to the audience but management does not want you to treat the topic. In this case, questions arise. What are the politics of getting an idea cleared? What are the consequences of this story? Even if a story does not have high interest, its consequences may make it an important one to write. Employees should know the company line or position even if they are not interested in it. Knowing the organization's position helps you to decide whether to give an audience what it wants or what it should have.

If you decide to write the story, give special attention to developing a good angle. An angle is simply a point of view that comes through clearly. It must go beyond simply writing about a topic like federal safety standards—one that can cure insomnia. You need an angle. A good angle for federal safety standards might deal with ways to handle and dispose of toxic wastes, which also scores high in consequences, especially if your company deals with toxic waste disposal.

If you've chosen a good angle, the next problem is to overcome writing errors caused by sloppy or incomplete research. To refresh yourself on PR writing research, review Chapter 4 of *PRW3e*. Focus first on your topic's background. Develop a broad data base, then narrow it and pursue in-depth information. Interview experts in the field you're writing about. You may get quotes to make a dishwater-dull topic into a shining, interesting article.

The article's lead must get the interest of readers and tell them what the story is about. It should state the article's central point. Readers won't devote much time searching for the central point. Don't bury it. Put it up front, and rely on the body of the story to hold onto the readers the lead has captured.

The body supports and explains the central point. It amplifies, interprets, verifies and illustrates. Use anecdotes to sustain interest by giving readers something to visualize. Anecdotes show readers instead of merely telling them. Anecdotes also humanize stories. And direct quotes make stories more personal and livelier. Both anecdotes and quotes also dramatize points.

Description is especially important when you're writing about something unfamiliar to your audience. Writing good description can be difficult. As a rule of thumb, describe the unfamiliar with the familiar. To say a microcomputer drives the new accounting system may be meaningless to many readers. If you write that the computer uses less than half the space on the top of an office desk, every reader has a clearer image. Everyone has seen an office desk.

Employee publications often copy the news release style of writing. That's not a bad tactic, but feature treatments usually make these publications more interesting to read than if copy is handled as hard news. And seldom is an employee publication issued often enough to justify the hard news approach. But if you use the feature treatment just to showcase your writing skills, you're missing the point.

Employees don't look at the style; they look at the substance. If you concentrate on learning what they want to know and use the feature approach to give it to them, they'll be glad to see each new edition. That's because you're giving them information they want in a format that is easy to understand. That should be your enduring purpose.

EXERCISES

SPECIAL NOTICE

It is acceptable in this assignment to create attribution and quotes as you need them, a fairly common practice in the field. However, common practice is also to clear all attributions and quotes by the persons named before stories are released.

Two different audiences are involved in the following assignments. Review your position paper or backgrounder carefully to pick up points of view that are especially relevant to each audience and feature those angles.

FNB 14 : 1

Use the position paper completed in Assignment 9:1 as the basis for doing a feature story for FNB's employee publication and one for the state's banking journal. Look carefully at the major points of the position paper. Evaluate the audiences that will read these stories. Orient your stories to those audiences.

NATS 14 : 1

Use the position paper completed in Assignment 9:1 as the basis for feature stories for a state trade magazine and one for a national magazine like the one published by the American Automobile Association. Your point of view should come through clearly: learning to prevent accidents at home and while driving is far more rewarding than time spent in an emergency room.

NCCC 14 : 1

Use the position paper completed in Assignment 9:1 as the basis for feature stories in a national magazine like *Parents* and one that is business oriented, such as the magazine produced by the U.S. Chamber of Commerce. Review your position paper carefully to glean information and points of view that are especially relevant to these diverse readers.

TEI 14 : 1

Use the backgrounder completed in Assignment 9:1 as the basis for feature stories to be run in a national law enforcement magazine and one in a national banking journal. Review the backgrounder carefully to gather information and points of view that are especially relevant to the readers of these two very different magazines.

Independent 14 : 1

Use the backgrounder completed in Assignment 9:1 as the basis for feature stories in the student newspaper and the university's alumni magazine. Examine the issue from the points of view of these diverse audiences and write specifically to them. Although each group of readers may be interested in the university, their interests are motivated by different concerns. Make sure you know these differences before you begin writing.

Notes -

Quick-Study 15

Extract, Chapter 15, "Speeches and Scripts," *Public Relations Writing: Form & Style* 3e, Belmont, California: Wadsworth, 1991

Writing speeches and scripts presents special challenges. You must deal with the combination of words, images and the performance element. You've no doubt had the experience of responding enthusiastically to a speech or an audiovisual show. Why?

The message seemed personal or was framed in terms you could understand or you liked the way it was delivered. Now think of the times when you were bored beyond description during a speech. What went wrong? One of the elements just described was no doubt missing.

Probably the most important key to effective speech and script writing is to research the topic thoroughly and prepare it for a specific audience. Audiences sense when they're given canned material, and they respond accordingly. They also sense when the message is tailored especially for them, and they like that care and attention.

Another point is to remember that you're preparing material to be delivered by someone else. So you must contend with two audiences. The first is an audience of one, the person who is to deliver the speech or voices the narration from a script. You must write a natural sounding speech or script. It also must have a comfortable rhythm and pace. Avoid tongue-twisting words and phrases and leave out the jargon. Although you may focus on the primary audience, if you forget that the audience of one is both message and medium, your message may not succeed, however good it is.

A third essential element in writing speeches and scripts is to find out what the audience already knows. Review current journal articles to find this out. Such a study also should tell you whether what you had planned to write is going to work with a particular audience. You must also research the person who will deliver the speech or read the narration. Note the person's patterns of speech, body language and the like. Use symbols important to the audience and appropriate for the speaker.

A fourth element is the effect you want to create for your audience. That will govern how you structure the message. Most messages are informational. Others are persuasive, entertaining or technical.

The nature of PR writing is that you routinely prepare materials for other people to use, so you can call on those skills to help you write speeches and scripts. However, even for highly skilled writers, this work can be hazardous duty. Professionals rise to the challenge.

Writing scripts for slides or video calls for a high level of visualization. Such scripts use monologues or dialogues with visuals. You must think about how to show what you say. Every paragraph, maybe every sentence, may call for distinct visuals to give context and add meaning to the message. That is a creative challenge.

Choosing a narrator for a slide or video script is much like casting for plays, television commercials or PSAs. You have some choice over who gets the role, so talent can, to some extent, be fitted to the script. But a speech must also be fitted to the person who gives it. Speeches and scripts must also be rehearsed to work out kinks in phrasing, pacing, timing and the like.

Not only must you write a speech, but you must also write an introduction of the speaker. Introductions should be tailored as carefully as the speeches themselves, but they must be brief. They should focus on whatever in the speaker's background is likely to be most interesting and suitable for the audience to hear. Leave out everything else. Even slide shows and videos need introductions. Here you'll concentrate on a brief statement that explains the presentation's purpose, who sponsors it and why it may be important to the audience.

EXERCISES

SPECIAL NOTICE

Review extensively the position paper or backgrounder you did as Assignment 9:1. Your assignment here is to do two pieces. One is a 10-minute speech. The other is a 6-minute audiovisual script. Each must stand alone, and yet each must work well with the other in case the speaker also wants to show the AV.

This assignment is not especially difficult, but you can fall into all sorts of traps unless you decide clearly ahead of time what will go into the speech and what will go into the AV. If possible, the speech should be set large type for easier reading. Time the speech, using an average rate of delivery to come up with a page count. For the AV, describe the content of the slides down the left side of the page and the narration down the right. Make sure they go together well.

FNB 15 : 1

The focus of the FNB speech and AV is to make the point that independent hometown banks provide better customer services because they are owned and run by people who are integral parts of the community. They are more likely to treat people like people, not numbers, to remember names and faces and to ask about a sick child. The whole atmosphere of an independent hometown bank is that of a "family and friends." The speech will be used to address a local service club next month. Of course, the AV can also be presented to public schools in the area, as well as to other interested groups.

TEI 15 : 1

The focus of the TEI speech and AV should be on the safety of using ATMs. TEI's president and marketing director expect to make this speech to many service clubs and professional groups around the area, as well as at some regional and national meetings. TEI also plans to make copies available free to TEI-customer banks that request it. It will sell the AV to nonTEI-customer banks at cost. Banks will be encouraged to use the AV in their local markets and schools.

NATS 15 : 1

The NATS leadership team, as well as its board of directors, has asked for a canned speech and AV presentation that members can give to local and statewide medical groups around the country. In fact, NATS expects to identify emergency care physicians in major markets and to rely on them as local coordinators who will seek out social and professional groups suitable for presentations. These coordinators will also arrange for medical personnel to visit their local schools for presentations and questions and answers. Look carefully at the types of audiences that may be reached and shape the speech and AV to fit their needs, at the same time making the point that it is better to prevent an accident than to treat it in an emergency context.

NCCC 15 : 1

Developmental child-care centers are good investments for more businesses. When employees know their children are getting not only good child care but developmental guidance at nominal costs, they are happier in their work and are more productive. That's the message you'll build into the speech and the AV you've been assigned to prepare for NCCC. The leadership at each NCCC center will be asked to speak to social, service and professional groups in their respective communities. They'll also make the AV available to public schools locally.

Independent 15 : 1

Refer to the backgrounder you did on the issue identified in Assignment 9:1. The director of student services on your campus has asked for a canned speech and AV she or he can use to present to appropriate campus and community groups. Consider the nature of these groups and pitch the speech and AV so they speak directly to those groups, while at the same time advocating a particular point of view.

Notes -

Quick-Study 16

Extract, Chapter 16, "Newsletters and Brochures," *Public Relations Writing: Form & Style* 3e, Belmont, California, Wadsworth, 1991

Although writing copy for newsletters and brochures is a common task in public relations work, it can be quite rewarding. That's because newsletters and brochures are often showpieces for firms. They are also important links to employees and other relevant groups.

Newsletters combine some qualities of newspapers and personal letters. Employee newsletters share information with employees and retirees. Although some employee newsletters are circulated to people outside an organization, they're really internal devices. The content is generally information-intensive, but it also has a personal touch intended to humanize the organization.

These newsletters are seldom issued at intervals short enough to deal with hard news. The best newsletters develop feature angles and rewrite hard news to freshen the stories and make them more interesting. Humor is often used to lighten the information in many employee newsletters. It's a good technique, but use it with caution. Most of us can't write like Art Buchwald or Erma Bombeck.

Special interest newsletters are legion. They include newsletters that appeal to life-style, economics, politics, religion, social and professional interests. Some serve only the membership of organizations. Others promote causes and issues. Still others operate as profit centers by selling specialized information to clients.

The writing style of newsletters ranges from formal to informal, but styles are always keyed to audience interests. Format may range from simple, inexpensive letter-size sheets to tabloid newspapers. Some are typed and reproduced on copy machines. Others are set in type and printed on costly stock. Art ranges from nonexistent to crude to elaborate. Budget governs how a newsletter is prepared and distributed. But it is also true that style, format, reproduction and distribution methods are less important to readers than content. If content meets audience needs, then your newsletter is successful—no matter how it looks.

Brochures are more fluid than newsletters. Unlike newsletters, brochures sell ideas, products, services or candidates. In this sense, brochure copy is more akin to advertising copy than to newsletter copy. Review Chapter 12 in *PRW3e* on advertising copywriting.

You begin a brochure by working out a clear *concept* for it. A brochure is both medium and message. Words, art, design, color, paper stock, size and distribution method must work together to convey the central idea clearly and persuasively. So the basic concept must be developed carefully and up front.

Suppose you must prepare a brochure for the Kenya Wildlife Fund, which works to stop the slaughter of elephants for their ivory. You can build the concept around KWF's need for money to combat poaching. Or, you might focus on the legal battles KWF has with poachers. Or, your concept might be a plea not to buy or wear ivory and to persuade friends to do the same. Any of these approaches and many others could be the brochure's primary concept.

Take special care to make the concept believable. Be selective with the facts used and arguments you make in the brochure. Use only information that validates the concept. Leave out everything else. Write brochure content as a unit. Hone and pare the message until it says exactly what you want it to say.

Then break it into parts and begin the design process. Design should always defer to content. Change content to fit design *only* if modifications don't harm content. A persistent problem with brochures is writing to fit available space. Copyfitting is sometimes an onerous task. Review Appendix C in *PRW3e* for some brief, easy-to-follow copyfitting procedures. If you're working on a desktop publishing system, the task is easier because you can instantly change such things as line length, spacing and typeface or size.

However, don't become blindly enthralled with desktop publishing systems. They can't do anything you can't do. If you can't write well, even the most sophisticated system won't improve your writing. If you can't design with pencil and paper, you can't design any better on a video screen.

With the right software, desktop systems can help you deal quickly and easily with late-breaking facts, check your spelling, improve your word choice, alert you to homophone misuses and some grammatical mistakes. They can also help you experiment quickly with a variety of formats, visual treatments, typefaces and sizes and line lengths. They can also speed up the copyfitting process. But to use these capabilities fully, you must practice them daily, something that isn't probable in most PR jobs.

EXERCISES

FNB 16 : 1

One step FNB must take as it prepares for the installation of the Money Machine 2001 on the campus at State University is to produce a brochure about the ATM. The brochure should explain to State University students (1) the benefits of using the Money Machine 2001 and (2) how to use it for all their transactions. FNB has asked ProCom to develop a brochure concept. FNB has also asked for a tentative design and some sample copy. Because you've worked so closely with FNB on this project, ProCom assigns you all these tasks.

FNB's only direct instructions are that " . . . We want to keep it simple. There should be some illustrations (photos or drawn art) to show step-by-step procedures for using the ATM. And the copy should be written to about the 10th grade level. We also want it to be small enough to insert in monthly statements, but, at the same time, we also want it designed so it can be used as a self-mailer. Choose a paper stock and ink color compatible with the bank's other printed materials. We would also consider the use of a second color, but you must justify the extra cost." Get the due date for this work from your supervisor at ProCom.

TEI 16 : 1

TEI management has been watching closely the usage patterns of the FNB ATM at State University. Early data seem to suggest the average value of transactions, mostly by students, is only about 48 percent of ATMs serving general populations across the country. FNB is delighted with these early data because they likely mean the ATM on the State University campus will be a good profit center.

TEI is pleased, too, but TEI's intent is to market its Money Machine 2001 to campuses around the country, in cooperation with local banks.

Its purpose is to sell machines. TEI is also aware of the brochure that FNB has produced to encourage ATM use and to explain its operations.

What TEI fears is that the early usage of the experimental machine at State University may later show a decline when students, the primary users, become more aware that it costs them a good bit more to do two separate $25 transactions rather than one $50 transaction. Because TEI is looking at the long-term implications of this experiment, it decides to develop a model brochure for the Money Machine 2001.

This brochure will become a tool in TEI's overall marketing scheme if it decides to go national with the plan. Rather than using the focus of the FNB brochure, TEI wants a model brochure that not only explains benefits and operations but also offers counsel about how users can manage wisely their resources when they use ATMs. This brochure, if it is approved, will be delivered to customer banks imprinted with their logo, address and phone number. TEI has asked ProCom to come up with a model brochure. It wants a concept, basic design and some sample copy.

ProCom assigns you these tasks. Unlike FNB, TEI has put no restrictions on the brochure. However, TEI has said it is most concerned about the brochure's strategy. It does not want to alienate FNB or future bank customers by producing a brochure that suppresses usage, but TEI believes that, in the long-term, it is in its interest, as well as that of customer banks, to encourage prudent customer use of ATMs. Get the due date ProCom has promised TEI for this model brochure.

NCCC 16 : 1

Review the position paper you did in Assignment 9:1. NCCC's experimental arrangement with State University seems to be working well. The center has been open for three months and was filled to capacity by the middle of the second month of operations.

Surveys show client families have high regard for the way their children are being cared for. Focus group interviews with parents have uncovered stories of positive changes in behavior of their children. A benchmark survey of students, staff and faculty about their child-care needs two months before the center opened showed a general lack of high regard for the services then available in Serene. Results of another survey released yesterday shows client families to be highly favorable toward the NCCC campus program.

Discussions with State University leaders have also been positive. And because there is already a long waiting list of potential clients, NCCC is considering expanding the State University facility, although no final decision has been been made. All the signs, however, have prompted NCCC management to look even harder at its long-range objective of developing centers on other campuses.

A basic step in marketing these centers on other campuses is to prepare a brochure that showcases the State University center and its success. NCCC wants ProCom to develop a basic concept for this brochure, along with a tentative design and some sample copy. It really isn't looking for a finished brochure because a decision to go national on this project is still a year or so away. NCCC simply wants to get its plan worked out in detail so that it can be implemented quickly and effectively if a positive decision is made. ProCom assigns you this task because you've worked so successfully on other NCCC projects. NCCC has imposed no restrictions.

The only instruction from Sully Trotter is that " . . . we want to do it right. We want to showcase this idea and make it so compelling that campus administrators will beat a path to our door, once they've seen our brochure." Because this is a speculative task for NCCC, check with your ProCom supervisor about the deadline.

NATS 16 : 1

The NATS leadership is committed to the idea that the best solution to the emergency medical care problem is to prevent the need for it. That's why NATS values so much the position paper you did as Assignment 9:1. But NATS is also realistic enough to know that even preventable accidents happen.

So NATS has asked ProCom to produce a brochure that details step-by-step procedures to be used until professional emergency medical specialists are on the scene. NATS wants this brochure to focus on nine trauma situations: (1) cardiac arrest, (2) automobile accidents, (3) poisoning, (4) burns, (5) smoke inhalation, (6) heat stroke, (7) drowning, (8) choking and (9) gunshot and stab wounds.

Because of the cost of printing and distributing millions of copies of this brochure, NATS wants it done in a single color on inexpensive stock. Although appearance is important, NATS is more concerned about content and the creative use of simple visuals to illustrate first-aid procedures.

Because this project will tax its resources, NATS has asked ProCom to develop a concept for the brochure, a tentative design and some sample copy. If there is a favorable review, the brochure will be fully developed and bids taken for its production. NATS is anxious to get an early look at what ProCom recommends. Check with your supervisor for a deadline.

Independent 16 : 1

Brochures are fairly common in the departments of many universities. They explain the nature of departmental programs and the personnel (faculty and staff) and facilities and equipment available to support these programs. The intent of most of these brochures, even if unstated, is to recruit students to these programs.

The situation at your University is an uneven mix of materials. Some departments have brochures. Some are elaborate. Others are quite modest. Your department has no brochure at the moment, but the head of the program wants one. Law prohibits use of state funds for brochures. So private funds must be used, and these are limited.

There is enough money to produce an 8.5" by 11" bifold brochure on plain stock, perhaps with a second color. The estimated press run is 5,000 copies. Because money is tight, the department head has asked around for names of people who could undertake this project. She or he has settled on you.

You should get a university catalog, a few brochures from other departments and some copies of memos and letters that talk about the objectives and philosophy that drive the department's programs. Using this information as a base, interview the department head and a sampling of faculty and students, probing for points of view, strengths and weaknesses and so on until you have a good feel for what should be put into the brochure. Develop a brochure concept. Then write and design it. Have it ready for client review by the time she or he sets.

Notes -

Quick-Study 17

Extract, Chapter 17, "Annual, Employee and Public Interest Reports," *Public Relations Writing: Form & Style* 3e, Belmont, California: Wadsworth, 1991

Publicly owned firms must issue annual reports, and federal requirements say these reports must be clear and accurate. Many other firms issue these reports because they think they should. But sometimes firms don't really want to explain clearly how they are doing, so they obscure the facts. Their reports may be technically accurate, but the writing is so burdened with conditional clauses and big words that hardly anyone knows or cares what they say.

One problem with the writing in annual reports is that the copy must be cleared through many levels and people. In the process, a simple, direct sentence or a whole article may get changed into a piece of fuzzy, indirect writing.

Annual reports are rarely assigned to inexperienced writers. You may help with an annual report in your first job, but your role will be limited to gathering basic information and the like. Although they are larger projects, preparing annual reports can be approached much as you would prepare a brochure.

Annual reports attempt two things: (1) to provide investors with basic data about firms and (2) to describe operations and prospects for the future. Annual reports are written for select audiences, but rarely for just one or two. Develop a complete list of audiences. Don't be surprised if you have a list of 20 or more names. Study the list carefully to determine which groups are essential to the success of your firm. Write your report to those few groups.

There is no absolute inventory of content for an annual report, but review Appendix B in *PRW3e* for some suggestions from Doremus Public Relations. A key element in an annual report is the *executive's letter*.

Another is the *narrative*, in which you tell the organization's story in detail. It should give a general description of the company or institution; its location, purposes, products and services; and its related activities. It should amplify what happened last year and project the future, even if the executive's letter mentions them. The narrative must also disclose and describe events, management decisions, sales, mergers or conditions that have had, or will have, important effects on operations.

The most successful annual reports often make strong thematic statements. A good theme can be the creative glue that binds diverse pieces of information. It also can give the impression that a firm is highly organized and managed well.

Annual reports may range from modest to elaborate, but their preparation and production stretch over several months. Commonly, six or seven months will elapse from the time of the first planning meeting until the annual report is distributed.

Two important variations of annual reports are now more common. They are *employee annual reports* (EARs) and *public interest reports* (PIRs).

Employee annual reports concentrate on the rationales behind management decisions. These reports give employees a keener sense of "ownership," a much needed sense of belonging, because of the mounting losses of employee identity and morale from merger-mania in the 1980s. Feelings of uncertainty about job security have also been aggravated by trends to greater globalization of markets and high bankruptcy rates.

Public interest reports help build and sustain corporate image and state socially responsible behavior. Although social issues may be mentioned, the legal purposes of annual reports greatly restrict space and time devoted to matters of public concern. Public interest reports fill this need. They try to show firms as socially accountable. They show how firms use natural resources in responsible ways, not just for their own purposes, but for the good of their communities. They sometimes focus on employees who take community leadership roles. They also provide forums in which companies can talk about how they are keeping faith with the public trust.

The primary targets of PIRs are *influentials*, individuals or groups whose support or opposition is important to the organization's success. They may head vast financial empires, serve on a regulatory board or they may be a small but vocal group of opponents. But all are people who influence policy decisions affecting the success of firms.

EXERCISES

FNB 17 : 1

Although FNB has never issued a public annual report, the bank's leadership has just adopted a policy that obligates it to issue a report annually. The philosophy behind this decision is that FNB leadership believes it has the responsibility to its customers, stockholders and stakeholders in the community to report on the bank beyond what shows up in the financial statements of condition published in the *Clarion* at the close of each quarter.

In a sense, this decision represents FNB's individual effort to counteract the negative attitudes toward all financial institutions as a result of so many recently failed banks and the savings and loan scandal. FNB is aware that its own report won't have any effect beyond its marketing territory, but it is determined to do what it believes is the "right thing to do for Serenites."

Olan Gable has often said, "We treat depositors' money as if it is our own. People do business with us because they trust us. Without their trust, FNB would die."

So the purposes of this first annual report are (1) to share the good news about the bank, (2) interpret economic trends in the community and (3) speculate on the future and explain how FNB expects to grow and develop with the community.

FNB has looked at the elaborate annual reports issued by some megabanks. Although FNB is willing to follow suit, its primary goal is to produce a report that is recognized and appreciated by its readers for its substance. FNB has turned over this project to ProCom. ProCom has promised to produce a thematic treatment, along with a rough design and some sample copy.

After ProCom management assigns this project to you, you decide the sample copy will be a draft of the president's letter. Your ProCom supervisor agrees with you. So review all the work you've done with FNB and develop the assignment.

NATS 17 : 1

NATS produces a slim annual report for its membership. This document usually focuses on NATS's financial status, membership trends and recent public policy changes affecting emergency medicine. Because NATS has become proactive by educating people about the benefits of preventing accidents as a way of minimizing the need for emergency care, it decided yesterday to issue a public interest report on the idea. Shortly after the NATS board made this decision, NATS called ProCom to explain the idea and to ask for ProCom's help.

A meeting is set between ProCom and NATS leadership next week for an initial discussion. Based on yesterday's phone call, your assignment is to conceptualize this public interest report, produce a draft design and write some sample copy for it. As this assignment requires a quick turnaround, you'll need to review all the materials you've produced to date for NATS as well as any pertinent library materials.

Next week's meeting with the NATS people will probably result in several changes in what you propose, but that's expected. Go into this assignment with the idea that what you produce will not get approval without significant change. Final approval may not come until several meetings are held and you've gone through several design and writing treatments. Check with your ProCom supervisor for a deadline.

NCCC 17 : 1

Because the experimental day-care center at State University has proved so successful, NCCC is planning similar centers on six other campuses. Serious negotiations are under way at 22 other campuses. Formal announcement of agreements with most or all of these institutions are expected within the next two or three months. Several other campus administrations have shown tentative interest, but it is too early to tell which way they'll go.

NCCC seems to be riding the crest of considerable public recognition and respect. Several prominent educational journals have carried stories about the Serene center's effectiveness. So have some popular magazines, including *Time*. Associated Press has also done a lengthy series carried in many of the nation's daily newspapers.

NCCC wants to exploit this environment, so it has decided to produce a public interest report (1) to persuade readers of the benefits to society for the type of centers NCCC is now operating at campus sites and (2) to establish NCCC as *the* leader in child-care developmental centers.

That shouldn't be difficult, given the kind of recent attention NCCC has gotten.

NCCC has turned, naturally, to ProCom to produce its public interest report. And NCCC has specifically asked that you undertake the project. ProCom agrees and suggests that you first develop a concept for the public interest report, write some sample copy for it and do a tentative design.

Your supervisor warns you not to get caught up in the euphoria surrounding NCCC's success at State University. Yes, there is a good story to tell, but stick with the facts. Facts seem to speak more persuasively than glittering generalities. NCCC has set no deadline on this assignment but your ProCom supervisor has a deadline in mind. Find out what it is.

TEI 17 : 1

TEI has always issued an annual report, but it has never produced an employee annual report. TEI is a diversified company, and some employees in other divisions are a little perplexed at the recognition their colleagues are getting as they market the Money Machine 2001 nationally on campuses in cooperation with local banks. There is some misunderstanding and maybe a little envy that the ATM people are getting so much attention.

Chase now thinks an employee annual report will improve employee understanding of TEI's diverse operations and improve morale in all divisions. If the first report does what Chase wants, it will become a regular feature of TEI's communications program. Chase talked with Professor yesterday. She explained the problem and her solution. Professor agreed that an employee report could help and promised to give Chase within a week a concept for the report, a tentative design and some sample copy to review.

Professor then assigns you the project because you've done so much work with TEI. Review some public interest reports and all materials you've written for TEI before you begin writing and designing the current project. Check with Professor about the deadline for having materials ready for an in-house discussion before your work is presented for TEI's consideration.

Independent 17 : 1

Conceptualize and write some sample copy, as well as create a basic design, for a public interest report on student government programs on your campus. Plan this report for distribution to the *whole* university community, not just to students.

Review the structure of student governance, the nature of student programs and services and how the student government mechanisms relate to overall University governance. A key component, too, is how student government is funded and how it spends those funds. You may find it useful to do in-depth interviews with student government leaders and the principal administrators at your university.

Notes -

Notes -

Appendix

The Standard Advertising Unit

Advertisers, especially those operating at regional or national levels, have often ignored newspapers in their media schedules because of the lack of standard column widths and page depths. This promoted the industry to introduce the Standard Advertising Unit in 1981. The SAU was refined and reintroduced, effective July 1, 1984. It is a simple system that defines a column inch as one column wide by one inch deep, where a column is 2.0625 (or 2 1/16) inches wide and there is .125 (or 1/8) inch between columns. Therefore, a 31.5 SAU ad can be 3x10.5 or 2x15.75 inches. By consulting the table below, a three column ad is 6.4375 inches or 38.625 picas wide by 10.5 inches or 63 picas deep. A two column ad is 4.25 inches or 25.5 picas by 15.75 inches or 94.5 picas deep.

The standard column width also helps newspapers use a modular page design. That's why only the widths and depths in the table below are recommended for modular-style newspapers. Of course, newspapers may accept ad sizes other than those in the table. For our purposes, use only recommended SAU sizes in all assignments.

The SAU system was developed primarily by the American Newspaper Publishers Association and the Newspaper Advertising Bureau. The system also was done with the support of and in consultation with the Association of National Advertisers, the American Association of Advertising Agencies and the International Newspaper Association of Marketing Executives. Other organizations that took part in deliberations include the ANPA-Research Institute, ANR, INCFO, INPA, Media Records, NASA, NNA, NRMA and SRDS.

Table of The Standard Advertising Unit (SAU)
All fractions are in decimals

Width in	1 Col.	2 Cols.	3 Cols.	4 Cols.	5 Cols.	6 Cols.	DT
Inches	2.0625	4.25	6.4375	8.625	10.8125	13.0	26.75
Picas	12.375	25.5	38.625	51.75	64.875	78.0	160.5

Depth in Inches							
1	1x1						
1.5	1x1.5						
2	1x2	2x2					
3	1x3	2x3					
3.5	1x3.5	2x3.5					
5.25	1x5.25	2x5.25	3x5.25	4x5.25			
7	1x7	2x7	3x7	4x7	5x7	6x7	
10.5	1x10.5	2x10.5	3x10.5	4x10.5	5x10.5	6x10.5	13x10.5
13*	1x13	2x13	3x13	4x13	5x13		
14	1x14	2x14	3x14	4x14	5x14	6x14	13x14
15.75	1x15.75	2x15.75	3x15.75	4x15.75	5x15.75		
18	1x18	2x18	3x18	4x18	5x18	6x18	13x18
21	1xFD**	2xFD**	3xFD**	4xFD**	5xFD**	6xFD**	13xFD**

* The 13-inch depth sizes may be used for tabloid sections in broadsheet newspapers.

** FD (full depth) can be 21 inches or deeper. Depths for each broadsheet newspaper are indicated in the Standard Rate and Data Service (SRDS).

Extrapolated from *Newpaper Rates and Data*, published by *Standard Rate and Data Service*, p. A16, October 12, 1991. *Used with permission.*